TRADE AND PROFESSIONAL ASSOCIATIONS IN CALIFORNIA

A Directory

Center for California Public Affairs

AN AFFILIATE OF THE CLAREMONT COLLEGES

Claremont

The Center for California Public Affairs, founded in 1969 and
affiliated with The Claremont Colleges, is a nonprofit foundation
for research, publishing, and public service. It is concerned
primarily with the character, problems, and future development
of California.

The Center is the leading publisher of reference books about California
and its problems. For a complete list of our publications, write:

CENTER FOR CALIFORNIA PUBLIC AFFAIRS
P.O. Box 10
Claremont, California 91711

(714) 624-5212

Copyright 1979, Center for California Public Affairs

Library of Congress Cataloging in Publication Data
Main entry under title:

Trade and professional associations in
   California.

   1. Trade and professional associations--
California--Directories. I. Center for
California Public Affairs.
HD2428.C3T73   016'.94'025   78-12999
ISBN 0-912102-37-3

INTRODUCTION

This is a directory of nonprofit business and professional associations located in California. It is limited to organizations of statewide or regional (northern or southern California) scope, national associations that have offices in the state, and a few local groups of statewide interest. Local and county chambers of commerce are excluded. In a few cases, we have listed bistate organizations headquartered in adjacent states, e.g., the Grapefruit Advisory Board in Phoenix.

Entries give the name of the organization, its address and telephone number, and a brief explanatory note when the nature of the organization is not obvious. If there is more than one principal office in California, we have tried to list all of them. If no telephone number is listed, none was available.

Listings are in alphabetical order and numbered. The index of subjects and key words, which begins on page 53, refers to entry numbers.

All of the information was checked carefully by mail or telephone with the groups listed. Organizations were identified through telephone directories, specialized reference books, major trade associations and chambers of commerce, state lobbyist registration records, and the files of the Center for California Public Affairs, which has a continuing program of collecting information about California associations.

This is the first reference of its kind available since the Directory of California Non-Profit Associations was issued in 1970 by the San Francisco Public Library. We have deliberately kept the book as simple as possible to make it easier to issue revised editions at fairly frequent intervals.

No directory of this type is ever complete or, in spite of all pains taken, without errors. We urge users to contribute to the next edition by sending us additions and corrections.

1
Academy of Country Music
P.O. Box 508
Hollywood 90028   213-462-2351
2
Academy of Master Wine Growers
26 O'Farrell St.
San Francisco 94108   415-362-5071
3
Academy of Motion Picture Arts and Sciences
8949 Wilshire Blvd.
Beverly Hills 90211   213-278-8990
4
Academy of Psychologists in Marital and Family
  Therapy
U.S. International University
10455 Pomerado Road
San Diego 92131   714-271-4300
5
Academy of Television Arts and Sciences
6363 Sunset Blvd., Suite 711
Hollywood 90028   213-465-1131
6
Academy of Television Arts and Sciences
735 Montgomery St., Suite 200
San Francisco 94111   415-392-8002
7
Accountants for the Public Interest
Fort Mason Center, Bldg. 310, 3rd Floor
San Francisco 94123   415-885-3306
8
Actor's Fund of America
6777 Hollywood Blvd.
Hollywood 90028   213-464-4171
9
Administrative Management Society
3250 Wilshire Blvd.
Los Angeles 90010   213-380-9057
10
Administrative Management Society
625 Market St.
San Francisco 94105   415-421-3050
11
Adult Film Society of America
1654 Cordova St.
Los Angeles 90007   213-731-7236
12
Advertising Club of Los Angeles
3105 Wilshire Blvd.
Los Angeles 90010   213-382-1228
13
Aerospace Electrical Society
P.O. Box 24BB3
Los Angeles 90024

14
Air Conditioning and Refrigeration Contractors
  Association of Southern California, Inc.
2200 S. Hill St.
Los Angeles 90007   213-748-8448
15
Airline Medical Directors Association
7300 World Way West
Los Angeles 90009   213-646-3223
16
Airline Pilots Association
433 Airport Blvd.
Burlingame 94010   415-347-6644
17
Air Transport Association of America
Western Regional Office
8939 S. Sepulveda Blvd., Suite 408
Los Angeles 90045
18
Agricultural Council of California
P.O. Box 1712
Sacramento 95814   916-443-4887
     (Members are farmer cooperatives.)
19
Agricultural Education Foundation
111 G. St., Suite 31
Davis 95616   916-756-2870
     (Leadership training for agriculturists.)
20
Agricultural Leadership Associates
P.O. Box 421
San Luis Obispo 92306   805-541-1446
     (Alumni group for 19 above.)
21
Agricultural Producers Labor Committee
600 S. Commonwealth Ave., Suite 212
Los Angeles 90005   213-385-5065
22
Alfalfa Seed Production Research Board
P.O. Box 943
Dinuba 93618   209-591-4792
23
Allied Dairymen, Inc.
P.O. Box 642
Lemoore 93245   209-924-4103
24
Allied Finance Adjusters Conference
P.O. Box 489
Stockton 95201   209-466-2821
25
Allied Telephone Companies Association
1500 W. 58th St.
Los Angeles 90062

26
Almond Board of California
P.O. Box 15920
Sacramento 95813   916-929-6505

27
American Academy of Asian Studies
134 Church St.
San Francisco 94114   415-863-4168

28
American Advertising Federation
50 California St., Suite 425
San Francisco 94111   415-421-6867
    (Umbrella group for advertising business.)

29
American Agents Alliance
260 S. Arroyo Pkwy.
Pasadena 91105   213-684-2560

30
American Apparel Manufacturers Association
Los Angeles   213-627-0925

31
American Arbitration Association
P.O. Box 57994
Los Angeles 90057   213-383-6516
    (Resolution of disputes of all kinds.)

32
American Astronautical Society
P.O. Box 28130
San Diego 92128   714-746-4005

33
American Association for Marriage and Family
  Therapy
225 Yale Ave.
Claremont 91711   714-621-4749

34
American Association for Maternal and Child
  Health
P.O. Box 965
Los Altos 94022   415-964-4575

35
American Association for the Advancement of
  Science - Pacific Division
Golden Gate Park
San Francisco 94104   415-752-1554

36
American Association of Advertising Agencies
8500 Wilshire Blvd.
Beverly Hills 90211

37
American Association of Cost Engineers
160 Sansome St.
San Francisco 94104   415-421-3184

38
American Association of Critical-Care Nurses
P.O. Box 5445
Orange 92667   714-639-8942

39
American Association of Electromyography
  and Electrodiagnosis
7010 Via Valverde
La Jolla 92037   714-454-3722
    (Electronic study and diagnosis of muscles.)

40
American Association of Foundations for
  Medical Care
P.O. Box 230
Stockton 95201   209-948-4550

41
American Association of Gynecological
  Laparoscopists
11239 S. Lakewood Blvd.
Downey 90241   213-862-8181
    (Examination of peritoneal cavity.)

42
American Association of Medical Assistants
California Chapter
731 Market St.
San Francisco 94103   415-777-2000

43
American Association of Presidents of Independent Colleges and Universities
c/o Pepperdine University
Malibu 90265   213-456-4277

44
American Association of University Professors
Western Regional Office
582 Market St.
San Francisco 94104   415-989-5430

45
American Auto Racing Writers and Broadcasters
  Association
c/o Dusty Brandel
922 N. Pass Ave.
Burbank 91505   213-842-7005

46
American Board of Internal Medicine - Merit
  Project
2340 Clay St.
San Francisco 94115   415-921-1052

47
American Board of Periodontology
School of Dentistry
University of Southern California
Los Angeles 90007   213-741-5255
    (Diseases of tissues supporting the teeth.)

48
American Bottled Water Association
1411 W. Olympic Blvd.
Los Angeles 90015   213-384-3177
  49
American Building Contractors Association
2476 Overland Ave.
Los Angeles 90064   213-559-6664
  50
American Chemical Society
California Section Office
2140 Shattuck Ave.
Berkeley 94704   415-848-0512
  51
American Chemical Society
1540 N. Hudson Ave.
Los Angeles 90028   213-469-7278
  52
American Cinema Editors
422 S. Western Ave.
Los Angeles 90020   213-384-0588
  53
American College of Emergency Physicians
California Chapter
9841 Airport Blvd., Suite 1124
Los Angeles 90045   213-776-1820
  54
American College of Probate Counsel
10964 W. Pico Blvd.
Los Angeles 90064   213-475-1200
  55
American College of Trial Lawyers
10889 Wilshire Blvd.
Los Angeles 90024   213-879-0143
  56
American Concrete Pumping Association
404 W. Jacaranda Pl.
Fullerton 92632   714-879-7759
  57
American Criminal Justice Association
4048 Marlow Ct.
Carmichael 95608   916-483-4021
    (Also known as Lambda Alpha Epsilon; an
    organizations of professionals in the field.)
  58
American Defense Preparedness Association
Los Angeles Chapter
P.O. Box 661
Altadena 91001   213-681-8021
  59
American Endodontic Association
1400 N. Harbor Blvd.
Fullerton 92635   714-870-5590
    (Specialized branch of dentistry.)

60
American Electronics Association
9841 Airport Blvd.
Los Angeles 90045   213-641-8910
  61
American Federation of Aviculture
P.O. Box 1125
Garden Grove 92642
    (Rearing of birds.)
  62
American Forest Institute
Regional Office
6255 Sunset Blvd., Suite 601
Los Angeles 90028   213-462-7278
    (Communications and education arm
    of the timber industry.)
  63
American Frozen Food Institute
1838 El Camino Real
Burlingame 94010   415-697-6835
  64
American Gas Association
1425 Grande Vista
Los Angeles 90023   213-261-8161
    (Branch laboratory for gas appliances.)
  65
American Gem and Mineral Suppliers
  Association
1052 W. Sixth St., Suite 334
Los Angeles 90017   213-481-0880
  66
American Gem Society
2960 Wilshire Blvd.
Los Angeles 90010   213-387-7375
    (Jewelers' trade association.)
  67
American Gold Association
P.O. Box 457
Ione 95640   209-274-2196
  68
American Guides Association
P.O. Box B
Woodland 95695   916-662-6824
  69
American Guild of Authors and Composers
6430 Sunset Blvd.
Hollywood 90028   213-462-1108
  70
American Hospital Association
830 Market St.
San Francisco 94102   415-433-2550

71
American Hypnotists' Association
1159 Green St., Suite 6
San Francisco 94109   415-775-6130
72
American Importers Association
Southern California Unit
700 Wilshire Blvd., Suite 430
Los Angeles 90017   213-627-0634
73
American Incense Manufacturers Association
2217 S. Pontius Ave.
Los Angeles 90064   213-272-6523
74
American Industrial Real Estate Association
5670 Wilshire Blvd., Suite 1120
Los Angeles 90036   213-933-5749
75
American Institute of Aeronautics and
  Astronautics
9841 Airport Blvd., Suite 800
Los Angeles 90045   213-670-6642
76
American Institute of Banking
19 N. Marengo Ave.
Pasadena 91101   213-793-2700
77
American Institute of Building Design
2730 Arden Way, Suite 138
Sacramento 95825   916-483-2423
    (Professional group of building designers,
    primarily not licensed architects.)
78
American Institute of Hypnosis
7188 Sunset Blvd., Suite 200
Los Angeles 90069   213-874-8775
79
American Institute of Interior Designers
8687 Melrose Ave.
Los Angeles 90069   213-652-6485
80
American Institute of Maintenance
P.O. Box 2068
Glendale 91209   213-244-1176
81
American Institute of Oral Biology
P.O. Box 481
South Laguna 92677   714-499-1286
82
American Institute of Real Estate Appraisers
Southern California Chapter
99 E. Magnolia Blvd., Suite 122
Burbank 91502   213-849-7331

83
American Institute of Steel Construction
215 Market St.
San Francisco 94105   415-495-3550
84
American Institute of Steel Construction
714 W. Olympic Blvd.
Los Angeles 90015   213-747-5501
85
American Insurance Association
465 California St.
San Francisco 94104   415-362-2170
86
American Iron and Steel Institute
508 16th St.
Oakland 94612   415-763-6751
87
American Management Associations
San Francisco Management Center
1275 Market St.
San Francisco 94103   415-552-9100
88
American Marketing Association
681 Market St.
San Francisco 94105   415-777-2966
89
American Marketing Association
Los Angeles Chapter
5900 Wilshire Blvd., Suite 1402
Los Angeles 90036   213-933-7337
90
American Medical Electroencephalographic
  Association
P.O. Drawer LL
Santa Barbara 93102   805-682-2621
    (Recording of electric currents in brain.)
91
American Medico-Legal Institute
800 W. First St.
Los Angeles 90012   213-489-1880
92
American Mosquito Control Association
5545 Shields Ave.
Fresno 93727   209-292-5329
93
American Mutual Insurance Alliance
Regional Office
160 Sansome St., Suite 1411
San Francisco 94104   415-362-0870
94
American Narcolepsy Association
P.O. Box 5846
Stanford 94305   415-591-7979
    (Treatment of uncontrolled desire for
    sleep.)

95
American Newspaper Publishers Association
5670 Wilshire Blvd.
Los Angeles 90036   213-933-8526
96
American Nutrition Society
405 S. Los Robles Ave.
Pasadena 91101   213-796-1790
97
American Orthopaedic Foot Society
237 Estudillo Ave.
San Leandro 94577   415-483-2500
98
American Physical Therapy Association
California Chapter
1225 8th St., Suite 335
Sacramento 95814   916-446-0069
99
American Plywood Association
P.O. Box 3536
Fremont 94538   415-657-5959
100
American Polygraph Association
5410 Wilshire Blvd.
Los Angeles 90036   213-933-7491
    (Lie detectors.)
101
American Production and Inventory Control
  Society
Los Angeles Chapter
626 N. Garfield Ave.
Alhambra 91802   213-282-7438
102
American Property Managers Association
981 S. Western Avenue
Los Angeles 90006   213-732-6147
103
American Right of Way Association
P.O. Box 76296
Los Angeles 90020   213-383-2117
104
American Social Health Association
260 Sheridan Ave., Suite 307
Palo Alto 94306   415-321-5134
105
American Society for Aesthetic Plastic Surgery
3956 Atlantic Ave.
Long Beach 90807   213-427-8898
106
American Society for Metals
Los Angeles Chapter
P.O. Box 109
Alhambra 91802   213-284-8590

107
American Society of Cinematographers
1782 N. Orange Dr.
Hollywood 90028   213-876-5080
108
American Society of Civil Engineers
171 Second Street
San Francisco 94105   415-546-6546
109
American Society of Composers, Authors, and
  Publishers
6430 W. Sunset Blvd.
Los Angeles 90028   213-466-7681
110
American Society of Engineers and Architects
511 Garfield Ave.
South Pasadena 91030   213-682-1161
111
American Society of Enologists
P.O. Box 411
Davis 95616   916-752-0385
    (Professional wine specialists.)
112
American Society of Hematology
c/o T.B. Bradley, M.D.
Veterans Administration Hospital, 151A
4150 Clement St.
San Francisco 94121   415-221-4810
    (Medical blood specialists.)
113
American Society of Irrigation Consultants
8100 Sedan Ave.
Canoga Park 91304   213-881-8512
114
American Society of Music Arrangers
P.O. Box 11
Hollywood 90028   213-874-9318
115
American Society of Plumbing Engineers
15233 Ventura Blvd., Suite 616
Sherman Oaks 91403   213-783-4845
116
American Society of Professional Estimators
4055 Wilshire Blvd., Suite 418
Los Angeles 90010   213-382-6476
117
American Society of Safety Engineers
3388 W. 8th St.
Los Angeles 90005   213-385-6461
118
American Society of Travel Agents
1533 Wilshire Blvd.
Los Angeles 90017   213-483-0950

119
American Society of Travel Agents
26 O'Farrell St.
San Francisco 94108   415-391-5159

120
American Society of Women Accountants
6464 Sunset Blvd.
Los Angeles 90049   213-466-8649

121
American Society of Zoologists
California Lutheran College, Box 2739
Thousand Oaks 91360   805-492-4055

122
American Statistical Association
Southern California Chapter
c/o Orville Allen
Rockwell Space Division
12214 Lakewood Blvd.
Downey 90241   213-922-1957

123
American Surgical Association
c/o J.V. Maloney, Jr., M.D.
School of Medicine
University of California
Los Angeles 90024   213-825-0856

124
American Trucking Associations
Western Office
1240 Bayshore Highway
Burlingame 94010   415-347-8184

125
American Tunaboat Association
1 Tuna Lane
San Diego 92101   714-233-6405

126
American Women in Radio and Television, Inc.
P.O. Box 3615
Los Angeles 90028   213-466-7225

127
Antique Appraisal Association of America
11361 Garden Grove Blvd.
Garden Grove 92640   714-530-7090

128
Apartment and Motel Association of California
3921 Wilshire Blvd.
Los Angeles 90020   213-388-6136

129
Apartment Owners Club of Southern California
720 S. Euclid Ave.
Anaheim 92802   714-778-4400

130
Apartment Owners Council
4057 Udall St.
San Diego 92107

131
Apricot Advisory Board
1295 Boulevard Way, Suite H
Walnut Creek 94595   415-937-3660

132
Apricot Producers of California
1762 Holmes St.
Livermore 94550   415-447-7660

133
Artichoke Advisory Board
P.O. Box 747
Castroville 95012   408-633-4411

134
Artists Equity Association
81 Leavenworth St.
San Francisco 94102   415-626-6808

135
Asian American Law Student Association
1440 W. Ninth St.
Los Angeles 90015   213-389-2616

136
Asian American Librarians Association
c/o Kobayashi
113 11th Avenue
San Francisco 94118   415-668-0093

137
Associated Cabinet Manufacturers Association
of San Francisco
1255 Post St.
San Francisco 94109   415-673-3850

138
Associated California Loggers
c/o Alan Clarke, Legislative Consultant
555 Capitol Mall, Suite 745
Sacramento 95814   916-441-5835

139
Associated Credit Bureaus of California, Inc.
P.O. Box 1291
San Mateo 94401   415-342-5716

140
Associated Drilling Contractors of California
1217 Mariemont Ave.
Sacramento 95825   916-485-2220

141
Associated Farmers of California
447 Sutter St., Rm. 811
San Francisco 94108   415-421-5654

142
Associated General Contractors of California
301 Capitol Mall, Suite 402
Sacramento 95814   916-444-6430

143
Associated Independent Owner-Operators, Inc.
17100 S. Norwalk Blvd.
Cerritos 90650   213-587-8437

144
Associated Master Barbers and Beauticians of
   America
4158 Mentone Ave.
Culver City 90230   213-836-6868

145
Associated Master Barbers and Hair Stylists
   of California
1647 Heritage Cir.
Anaheim 92804   714-774-1369

146
Associated Meat and Food Suppliers of
   Southern California
6055 E. Washington Blvd., Suite 416
Los Angeles 90040   213-725-1064

147
Associated Produce Dealers and Brokers of
   Los Angeles
746 S. Central Ave.
Los Angeles 90021   213-623-6293

148
Associated Roofing Contractors of Northern
   California
1900 Point West Way, Suite 120
Sacramento 95815   916-929-2138

149
Associated Roofing Contractors of the Bay Area
   Counties, Inc.
8301 Edgewater Drive
Oakland 94621   415-635-8800

150
Associated Sandblasting Contractors Association
606 N. Larchmont Blvd.
Los Angeles 90004   213-467-1158

151
Associated Surplus Dealers
P.O. Box 480008
Los Angeles 90048   213-680-0176

152
Associated Tile Contractors of Southern Calif.
c/o Manny Fleishman
Fleishman Tile Company, Inc.
2736 S. La Cienega Blvd.
Los Angeles 90034   213-870-7826

153
Association for Contemporary Electronics
100 N. Winchester Blvd.
Santa Clara 95050   408-247-6331

154
Association for Humanistic Psychology
325 Ninth St.
San Francisco 94103   415-626-2375

155
Association for Systems Management
No address available   213-623-1970

156
Association for Transpersonal Psychology
P.O. Box 3049
Stanford 94305   415-327-2066

157
Association of Applied Insect Ecologists
10202 Cowan Heights Dr.
Santa Ana 92705   714-838-1550

158
Association of Aviation Psychologists
3982 San Bonito
Los Alamitos 90720   213-430-5648

159
Association of California Community College
   Administration
21250 Stevens Creek Blvd.
Cupertino 95014

160
Association of California Insurance Companies
11th and L Building
Sacramento 95814   916-442-4581

161
Association of California Life Insurance
   Companies
3055 Wilshire Blvd.
Los Angeles 90010   213-385-8892

162
Association of California Life Insurance
   Companies
1400 K Street
Sacramento 95814   916-442-3648

163
Association of California School Administrators
   Legislative Office
1517 L Street
Sacramento 95814   916-444-3216

164
Association of College Unions-International
P.O. Box 7286
Stanford 94305   415-328-8017
   (Campus community centers and activities.)

165
Association of Data Center Owners and Managers
P.O. Box 7623
Van Nuys 91409   213-988-5670

166
Association of Defense Counsel
943 Mills Building
San Francisco 94104   415-392-1676
167
Association of Electronic Distributors
9363 Wilshire Blvd., Suite 217
Beverly Hills 90210   213-278-0543
168
Association of Elementary School Administrators
12444 Victory Blvd.
North Hollywood 91606   213-877-8288
169
Association of Independent California Colleges
   and Universities
37 Brookhollow Dr.
Santa Ana 92705   714-546-7770
170
Association of Motion Picture and Television
   Producers
8480 Beverly Blvd.
Hollywood 90048   213-653-2200
171
Association of Pediatric Oncology Nurses
c/o Lorraine Bivalec, Pediatric Oncology
Pacific Medical Center
P.O. Box 7999
San Francisco 94120   415-563-8777
172
Association of Professional Ball Players of
   America
337 E. San Antonio Dr., Suite 203
Long Beach 90807   213-423-5258
173
Association of Professional Baseball Physicians
400 29th St.
Oakland 94609
174
Association of Professional Personnel Agencies
3807 Wilshire Blvd.
Los Angeles   213-387-9690
175
Association of Railway Museums
11226 Long Beach Blvd.
Lynwood 90262
176
Association of Specialized Machine Shops
2691 W. 9th St.
Los Angeles 90006   213-387-3278
177
Astronomical Society of the Pacific
1290 24th Ave.
San Francisco 94122   415-661-8660
   (For both professionals and amateurs.)

178
Auto Dismantlers Association of Southern
   California
535 E. Vine
West Covina 91790   213-337-8215
179
Automatic Transmission Rebuilders Association
6663 Ventura Ave., Suite A
Ventura 93003   805-643-4974
180
Automotive Maintenance and Garage Association
149 California St.
San Francisco 94111   415-362-8892
181
Automotive Service Council
4106 1/2 Norse Way
Long Beach 90808   213-420-2439
182
Avocado Advisory Board
4533 Mac Arthur Blvd., Suite B
Newport Beach 92660   714-540-8180
183
Avocado Growers Bargaining Council
P.O. Box 151
Fallbrook 92028   714-728-6004
184
Bay Area Construction Opportunity Program
   (BACOP)
367 2nd St.
Oakland 94607   415-451-6628
   (Affirmative action apprenticeship for
   minority groups.)
185
Bay Area Counties Roofing Industry Promotion
   Fund
8301 Edgewater Dr.
Oakland 94621   415-635-8800
186
Bay Area League of Industrial Associations
3640 Grand Ave.
Oakland 94610   415-893-1982
187
Bay Area Purchasing Council
215 Market St.
San Francisco 94105   415-543-5545
188
Better Business Bureaus
See local telephone directories. See also:
   Council of Better Business Bureaus.
189
Biomedical Engineering Society
P.O. Box 2399
Culver City 90230   213-789-3811

190
Blue Anchor, Inc.
730 Howe Ave.
Sacramento 95813   916-929-3050
   (Marketing cooperative for California and
   Arizona deciduous fruits.)
191
Bowling Proprietors of Southern California
1830 W. 8th St.
Los Angeles 90057   213-385-3011
192
Brazil - California Trade Association
350 S. Figueroa St.
Los Angeles 90071   213-627-0634
193
Brick Institute of America
55 New Montgomery
San Francisco 94105   415-781-7642
194
British American Chamber of Commerce and
   Trade Center
350 S. Figueroa St.
Los Angeles 90071   213-622-7124
195
Building Industry Association of California
1571 Beverly Blvd.
Los Angeles 90026   213-625-5771
196
Building Industry Credit Association
2351 W. Third St.
Los Angeles 90057   213-382-7151
197
Building Owners and Managers Association
700 S. Flower St.
Los Angeles 90017   213-624-2181
198
Building Owners and Managers Association
300 Lakeside Dr.
Oakland 94612   415-893-8780
199
Business Forms Management Association
6204 N. Delano Ave.
Fresno 93711   209-431-2647
200
Business and Professional Association of Los
   Angeles
P.O. Box Q
Beverly Hills 90213   213-935-3834
201
Business and Professional Employers
   Association of California
No address available   415-451-7891

202
Cabinet and Fixture Manufactures Guild
1255 Post St.
San Francisco 94109   415-673-3850
203
Calavo Growers of California
P.O. Box 3486, Terminal Annex
Los Angeles 90051   213-587-4291
204
Cal - Dari
318 Meedham St.
Modesto 95353   209-522-3241
205
Cal - Freestone Peach
P.O. Box 3004
Modesto 95353   209-524-6231
206
California Academy of Family Physicians
9 First St.
San Francisco 94105   415-982-6091
207
California Academy of Registered Dental
   Assistants
925 L St., Suite 850
Sacramento 95814   916-442-3555
208
California Advisory Board of Surety Agents
925 L St., Suite 220
Sacramento 95814   916-441-1972
209
California Aircraft Dealers Association
408 Forum Building
Sacramento 95814   916-444-5520
210
California Air Tanker Operators Association
3250 North Shingle Rd.
Shingle Springs 95682   916-422-5196
211
California Agricultural Aircraft Association
1107 9th St., Suite 900
Sacramento 95814   916-442-1819
212
California Agricultural Marketing Association
2855 Telegraph Ave.
Berkeley 94705   415-644-7105
213
California Almond Growers Exchange
18th and C Sts.
P.O. Box 1768
Sacramento 95808   916-442-0771
214
California Ambulance Association
1401 21st St.
Sacramento 95814   916-443-5959

215
California Apartment Association
601 N. Vermont Ave., Suite 202
Los Angeles 90004   213-380-7150
216
California Apartment and Motel Managers
  Association
2007 Wilshire Blvd.
Los Angeles 90057   213-483-2321
217
California Applicants Attorneys Association
331 J St., Suite 170
Sacramento 95814   916-446-7701
    (Attorneys representing claimants in
    workmen's compensation matters.)
218
California Apricot Advisory Board
1295 Boulevard Way, Suite H
Walnut Creek 94595   415-937-3660
219
California Artichoke Advisory Board
P.O. Box 747
Castroville 95012   408-426-2782
220
California Asparagus Growers Association
P.O. Box 1762
Stockton 95201   209-465-3482
221
California Asphalt Pavement Association
12501 Chandler Blvd., Suite 103
P.O. Box 4456
North Hollywood 91607   213-877-5241
222
California Assessment Bond Underwriters
  Association
311 California St., Suite 700
San Francisco 94104   415-391-0268
223
California Association for Private Education
925 L St.
Sacramento 95814   916-481-1922
224
California Association of Attorney - Certified
  Public Accountants
3750 W. 6th St.
Los Angeles 90020   213-382-5209
225
California Association of Catholic Hospitals
926 J St., Suite 1107
Sacramento 95814   916-444-3386
226
California Association of Childrens Hospitals
51st and Grove
Oakland 94609   415-654-5600

227
California Association of Children's Residen-
  tial Centers
1127 11th St., Suite 812
Sacramento 95814   916-446-0241
228
California Association of Collectors
1107 9th St., Room 529
Sacramento 95814   916-442-0366
229
California Association of Dispensing Opticians
1980 Mountain Blvd.
Oakland 94611   415-339-8151
230
California Association of Employers
140 Geary St.
San Francisco 94108   415-982-6901
231
California Association of Grower Gins, Inc.
P.O. Box 114
Raisin City 93652
232
California Association of Health Facilities
Headquarters
1401 21st St., Suite 202
Sacramento 95814   916-444-7600
233
California Association of Health Facilities
Regional Office
5225 Wilshire Blvd.
Los Angeles 90036   213-938-2644
234
California Association of Highway Patrolmen
2030 V St.
Sacramento 95818   916-452-6751
235
California Association of Homes for the Aging
926 J St.
Sacramento 95814   916-446-7633
236
California Association of Human Services
  Technologists
11th and L Building, Suite A
Sacramento 95814   916-444-2452
237
California Association of Independent Business,
  Inc.
201 - 203 S. Fern Ave.
Ontario 91761   714-984-6424
238
California Association of Independent News
  Distributors
25 Kearny St., Suite 300
San Francisco 94108   415-433-1025

239
California Association of Licensed Investigators
661 N. Arrowhead Ave.
San Bernardino 92401 714-884-1610

240
California Association of Life Underwriters
220 Montgomery St.
San Francisco 94104 415-397-2883

241
California Association of Medical Laboratory
 Technologists
1624 Franklin
Oakland 94612 415-893-5278

242
California Association of Nurserymen
1419 21st St.
Sacramento 95814 916-448-2881

243
California Association of Port Authorities
2230 K St.
Sacramento 95816 916-444-7158

244
California Association of Real Estate Brokers
2306 W. 79th
Inglewood 90305 213-758-0114

245
California Association of Realtors
505 Shatto Pl.
Los Angeles 90020 213-380-7190

246
California Association of Realtors
1129 10th St.
Sacramento 95814 916-444-2045

247
California Association of Rehabiliation
 Facilities
1225 18th St.
Sacramento 95814 916-441-5844

248
California Association of Resident Care Homes
2530 J St., Suite 302
P.O. Box 160274
Sacramento 95816 916-447-8885

249
California Association of School Psychologists
 and Psychometrists
180 El Camino Real
Millbrae 94030 415-697-9672

250
California Association of Schools of
 Cosmetology
606 N. Larchmont Blvd.
Los Angeles 90004 213-467-1158

251
California Association of Small Business
4440 Rainier Ave.
San Diego 92120 714-283-6018
 (Political action for small businesses.)

252
California Association of Thrift and Loan
 Companies
Drawer F
Redwood City 94063 415-365-1050

253
California Association of Tobacco and Candy
 Distributors
1224 Sheridan Rd.
Concord 94518 415-689-5025

254
California Association of Tobacco and Candy
 Distributors
1225 8th St.
Sacramento 95814 916-446-7841

255
California Association of Winegrape Growers
926 J St.
Sacramento 95814 916-441-1455

256
California Association of Sheet Metal and Air
 Conditioning Contractors
1434 Howe Ave., Suite 95
Sacramento 95825 916-920-4326

257
California Attorneys for Criminal Justice
6430 W. Sunset Blvd., Suite 521
Los Angeles 90028 213-462-1267
 (Criminal defense bar association.)

258
California Auto Body Association
3871 Piedmont Ave.
Oakland 94611 415-654-4445

259
California Automatic Vendors Association, Inc.
10889 Wilshire Blvd., Room 1400
Los Angeles 90024 213-477-5547

260
California Automotive Wholesalers' Association
2222 Sierra Blvd., Suite 22
Sacramento 95825 916-929-9621

261
California Avocado Board
4533 MacArthur Blvd., Suite B
Newport Beach 92660 714-540-8180

262
California Ayrshire Breeders Association
13520 Highway 128
Calistoga 94515 707-942-6619

263
California Bankers Association
650 California St.
San Francisco 94108   415-433-1894
264
California Barber College Association, Inc.
320 Pine Ave., Suite 610
Long Beach 90802   213-437-6427
265
California Bean Growers Association
P.O. Box 512
Oxnard 93032   805-483-2261
266
California Beef Cattle Improvement Associa-
tion
145 Animal Science Building
University of California
Davis 95616   916-752-1259
267
California Beef Council
1436 Rollins Rd.
Burlingame 94010   415-348-3171
268
California Beef Shorthorn Association
Route 1, Box 34
Byron 94514   209-835-5403
269
California Beer Wholesalers Association
1127 11th St., Room 806
Sacramento 95814   916-441-5402
270
California Beet Growers Association
2 W. Swain Rd.
Stockton 95207   209-477-5596
271
California Brandy Advisory Board
235 Montgomery St., Room 411
San Francisco 94104   415-398-0220
272
California Brewers Association
235 Montgomery St.
San Francisco 94104   415-421-7747
273
California Broadcasters Association
1107 9th St., Suite 907
Sacramento 95814   916-444-2237
274
California Building Industry Association
1225 8th St., Suite 500
Sacramento 95814   916-443-7933

275
California Building Material Dealers Association
99 E. Magnolia
Burbank 91502   213-849-5549
276
California Business Properties Association
c/o Hahn Inc.
P.O. Box 942
El Segundo 90245   213-772-4200
277
California Business Services Council
4057 Udall St.
San Diego 92107
278
California Canners and Growers
3100 Ferry Building
San Francisco 94106   415-981-0101
279
California Canning Peach Association
3708 Mt. Diablo Blvd., Suite 220
Lafayette 94549   415-284-9171
280
California Canning Pear Association
100 Bush St.
San Francisco 94104   415-982-3000
281
California Cattle Feeders Association
3040 19th St., Suite 6
Bakersfield 93301   805-327-3022
282
California Cattlemen's Association
1005 12th St., Suite A
Sacramento 95814   916-444-0845
283
California Celery Research Advisory Board
200 New Stine Rd., Suite 131
Bakersfield 93303   805-834-6575
284
California Charolais Association
P.O. Box 89
Keene 93531   805-854-2065
285
California Charter Bus Association
851 E. Cerritos
Anaheim 92805   714-776-9210
286
California Chiropractic Association
2201 Q St.
Sacramento 95816   916-443-6601
287
California Christmas Tree Growers
2855 Telegraph Ave.
Berkeley 94705   415-644-7086

288
California Chrysanthemum Growers Association
788 San Antonio Rd.
Palo Alto 94303   415-494-1451
289
California Coin-op Association
22152 Jonesport Ln.
Huntington Beach 92646   714-963-5976
290
California Collateral Loan Association
65 Post St.
San Jose 95113   408-205-1488
291
California Commercial Fisherman's Association, Inc.
P.O. Box 3017
Seal Beach 90740
292
California Conference of Employer Associations
923 12th St.
P.O. Box 1138
Sacramento 95805   916-443-1602
293
California Conference of Mason Contractor Associations, Inc.
2550 Beverly Blvd.
Los Angeles 90057   213-388-0476
294
California Conference of Mason Contractor Associations, Inc.
7844 Madison Ave., Suite 153
Sacramento 95621   916-966-7666
295
California Contemporary Fashion Guild
110 E. 9th St.
Los Angeles 90015   213-628-6100
296
California Contract Security Guard Association
8001 Capwell Dr.
Oakland 94621   415-638-2171
297
California Contractors Council, Inc.
1300 Ethan Way
Sacramento 95825   916-929-4384
298
California Cooperative Almond Hullers Association
P.O. Box 191
Ballico 95303   209-394-7941

299
California Cooperative Rice Research Foundation, Inc.
P.O. Box 306
Biggs 95917   916-868-5481
300
California Copyright Conference
6381 Hollywood Blvd.
Los Angeles 90028   213-463-7178
301
California Corn Growers, Inc.
Route 2 P.O. Box 184
Dos Palos 93620   209-387-4121
302
California Correctional Officers Association
510 Bercut Dr., Suite U
Sacramento 95814   916-447-8565
303
California Cosmetologists Association, Inc.
526 Mission St.
South Pasadena 91030   213-441-4228
304
California Cosmetology Legislative and Educational Committee, Inc.
4522 S. Western Ave.
Los Angeles 90062   213-569-5689
305
California Cotton Ginners Association
20900 Elgin Ave.
Lemoore 93245
306
California Council, American Institute of Architects
1736 Stockton
San Francisco 94133   415-986-0759
307
California Council for International Trade
1333 Gough, Suite 6-F
San Francisco 94109   415-982-6498
308
California Council of Air Conditioning and Refrigeration Contractors Association
1110 2nd St.
Sacramento 95814   916-444-3770
309
California Council of Air Conditioning and Refrigeration Contractors Association
2220 S. Hill St.
Los Angeles 90007   213-748-8448
310
California Council of Civil Engineers and Land Surveyors
1107 9th St., Room 811
Sacramento 95814   916-444-3060

311
California Council of Civil Engineers and Land
  Surveyors
608 Hill St., Suite 1010
Los Angeles 90014   213-624-7761

312
California Council of Independent Oil Companies
1118 10th St.
Sacramento 95814

313
California Council of Landscape Architects
4215 Freeport Blvd.
Sacramento 95822   916-452-4205

314
California Court Reporters Association
1107 9th St., Suite 626
Sacramento 95814   916-441-3787

315
California Cowboys Association, Inc.
7160 Forbes Rd.
Lincoln 95648   916-645-2644

316
California Creamery Operators, Inc.
P.O. Box 36
Davis 95616

317
California Credit Merchants Association
1543 W. Olympic Blvd.
Los Angeles 90015   213-387-0697

318
California Credit Union League
2322 S. Garey Ave.
Pomona 91766   714-628-6044

319
California Credit Union League
7700 Edgewater Dr.
Oakland 94621   415-562-7625

320
California Crop Improvement Association
University of California
Davis 95616   916-752-0544

321
California Dairy Herd Improvement Associa-
  tion
149 Animal Science Building
University of California
Davis 95616   916-752-6620

322
California Dairy Industries Association
P.O. Box 255463
Sacramento 95825   916-489-1391

323
California Dairymens Association
P.O. Box 53
Riverside 92502

324
California Dairy Museum and Educational
  Foundation
2775 Cottage Way, Suite 19
Sacramento 95825   916-445-8790

325
California Date Administrative Committee
81855 Highway III, Room 2-G
Indio 92201   714-347-4510

326
California Date Growers Association
P.O. Box HHH
Indio 92201   714-347-3304

327
California Dental Association
P.O. Box 91258
Los Angeles 90009   213-776-4292

328
California Dental Laboratory Association
2352 W. 3rd.
Los Angeles 90057   213-383-1228

329
California Dental Legislative Office
925 L, Suite 800
Sacramento 95814   916-444-2147

330
California Dining and Beverage Association
2555 E. Chapman, Suite 600
Fullerton 92631   714-738-1061

331
California District Attorneys Association
P.O. Box 7736, Rincon Annex
San Francisco 94120   415-864-9800

332
California Dried Fig Advisory Board
P.O. Box 709
Fresno 93712   209-264-5011

333
California Dried Fruit Export Association
303 E. Brokaw Rd. S.
Santa Clara 95052   408-241-9302

334
California Dry Bean Advisory Board
P.O. Box 943
Dinuba 93618   209-591-4866

335
California Dump Truck Owners Association
16610 E. Gale Ave.
Industry 91745   213-961-4491

336
California Electric Sign Association
100 S. Ellsworth
San Mateo 94401   415-343-9652
337
California Electric Sign Association
311 N. Normandie Ave.
Los Angeles 90004   213-666-5111
338
California Employment Association
P.O. Box 868
Arnold 95223   213-763-6226
339
California Escrow Association
6777 Hollywood Blvd., Suite 605
Los Angeles 90028   213-461-7383
340
California Escrow Institute
1900 State Street
Santa Barbara 93101   805-966-3991
341
California Fabricare Institute
10615 S. De Anza Blvd.
Cupertino 95014   408-252-1746
342
California Farm Bureau Federation
2855 Telegraph Ave.
Berkeley 94705   415-644-7105
343
California Farm Bureau Federation Political
  Action Committee (FARM PAC)
1127 11th St.
Sacramento 95814   916-443-7951
344
California Farmers
22651 Mt. Eden Rd.
Saratoga 95070   408-867-9198
345
California Fashion Creators
110 E. 9th St., Suite A-361
Los Angeles 90015   213-627-1034
346
California Fertilizer Association
222 Watt Ave.
Sacramento 95825   916-483-6027
347
California Fig Institute
P.O. Box 709
Fresno 93712   209-264-5011
348
California Fire Chiefs Association
6439 Floren-Perkins Rd.
P.O. Box 28147
Sacramento 95828   916-383-7927

349
California Fisheries Association
321 E. 2nd St., Suite 403
Los Angeles 90012   213-628-6966
350
California Food Producers, Inc.
717 K St., Suite 306
Sacramento 95814   916-441-0992
351
California Forest Communicators Council
1127 11th St., Suite 534
Sacramento 95814   916-444-6592
352
California Forest Protective Association
1127 11th St., Room 534
Sacramento 95814   916-444-6592
353
California Franchisee Council
50 California St., Suite 955
San Francisco 94111   415-981-4938
354
California Funeral Directors Association
2617 K St., Room 8
Sacramento 95816   916-442-3617
355
California Furniture Manufactures Association
1933 S. Broadway
Los Angeles 90007   213-747-9224
356
California Goat Dairymen's Association
P.O. Box 934
Turlock 95380   209-632-2821
357
California Grain and Feed Association
510 Bercut Dr., Suite H
Sacramento 95814   916-441-2272
358
California Grape and Tree Fruit League
1630 E. Shaw Ave., Suite 150
Fresno 93710   209-226-6330
359
California Green Lima Bean Growers
2855 Telegraph Ave.
Berkeley 94705   415-644-7086
360
California Grocers Association
400 S. El Camino Real, Suite 795
San Mateo 94402   415-344-1707
361
California Grocers Association
1131 L St.
Sacramento 95814   916-444-5545

362
California Growers Foundation
1108 Adams St.
St. Helena 94574   707-963-7191
    (Labor relations group.)
363
California Hampshire Sheep Breeders
  Association
Route 1, Box 222
Orland 95963   916-865-3024
364
California Harness Horse Breeders Associa-
tion
1047 S. Prairie Ave., Suite 3
Inglewood 90301   213-674-2261
365
California Highway Users Conference
926 J St.
Sacramento 95814   916-443-5314
366
California Holstein - Fresian Association
1274 W. Hedges, Unit 103
Fresno 93728   209-441-1206
367
California Home Furnishings Council
1933 S. Broadway, Room 244
Los Angeles 90007   213-749-6197
368
California Homemakers Association
5322 San Pablo Ave.
Oakland 94608   415-653-7020
369
California Horse Racing Association
P.O. Box 5050
San Mateo 94402   415-341-1067
370
California Hospital Association
925 L St., Suite 1250
Sacramento 95814   916-443-7401
371
California Hotel and Motel Association
520 Capitol Mall, Suite 706
Sacramento 95814   916-444-5780
372
California Housing Council
1777 Borel Pl., Room 415
San Mateo 94402   415-349-4252
373
California Independent Mortgage Brokers
  Association
2641 W. Olympic Blvd.
Los Angeles 90006   213-386-7383

374
California Independent Oil Marketers Associa-
tion
555 Capitol Mall, Suite 655
Sacramento 95814   916-441-5166
375
California Inland Pilots Association
Pier 9
San Francisco 94111   415-421-5678
376
California Insurance Association
14114 Victory Blvd.
Van Nuys 91401   213-988-9500
377
California Jaycees
412 Park Ave.
San Jose 95110   408-286-4620
    (Formerly: Junior Chamber of Com-
    merce.)
378
California Jewelers Association
606 S. Olive St.
Los Angeles 90014   213-628-3171
379
California Judges Association
2150 Shattuck Ave., Suite 817
Berkeley 94704   415-843-7118
380
California Land Surveyors Association
P.O. Box 7400
Santa Rosa 95401   707-526-2572
381
California Land Title Association
1024 10th St.
Sacramento 95814   916-444-2647
382
California Lathing and Plastering Contractors
  Association
3558 W. 8th St.
Los Angeles 90005   213-383-1281
383
California Legislative Conference of the
  Plumbing, Heating and Piping Industry
1434 Howe Ave., Suite 92
Sacramento 95825   916-929-1817
384
California Legislative Council of Professional
  Engineers
1127 11th St., Suite 900
Sacramento 95814   916-444-8274
385
California Library Association
717 K St.
Sacramento 95814   916-447-8541

386
California Licensed Beverage Association
508 16th
Oakland 94612   415-451-2377
    (Formerly: United Tavern Owners, Inc.)
387
California Licensed Contractors Association
1017 N. La Cienega Blvd.
Los Angeles   213-657-6110
388
California Licensed Vocational Nurses Asso-
    ciation, Inc.
912 Linley
Torrance 90502   213-320-6301
389
California Licensed Vocational Nurses Asso-
    ciation, Inc.
1617 Webster St.
Oakland 94612   415-452-4033
390
California Livestock Marketing Association
    (Ceased operations in 1978)
391
California Lumbermen's Accident Prevention
    Association
926 L St.
Sacramento 95814   916-444-8249
392
California Macadamia Society
P.O. Box 666
Fallbrook 92028   714-295-7022
393
California Manufactured Housing Association
1107 9th St., Suite 700
Sacramento 95814   916-446-4024
394
California Manufacturers Association
P.O. Box 1138
Sacramento 95805   916-441-5420
395
California Marine Parks and Harbor Associa-
    tion
408 Forum Building
Sacramento 95814   916-444-5520
396
California Medical Association
731 Market St.
San Francisco 94103   415-777-2000
397
California Medical Association
3345 Wilshire Blvd., Suite 50
Los Angeles 90010   213-380-8272

398
California Medical Association
925 L St.
Sacramento 95814   916-444-5532
399
California Metal Trades Association
1671 The Alameda
San Jose 95126   408-297-5522
400
California Milk Producers
1107 E. Artesia Blvd.
Artesia 90701   213-865-1291
401
California Milk Producers Advisory Board
1213 13th St.
Modesto 95352   209-521-1060
402
California Mining Association
P.O. Box 3
Jackson 95642   209-223-1129
403
California Mortgage Bankers Association
3440 Wilshire Blvd., Suite 1115
Los Angeles 90010   213-380-1486
404
California Motel Association
1713 J
P.O. Box 15556
Sacramento 95813   916-922-3110
405
California Motorcycle Dealers Association
3972 N. Waterman Ave., Room 106
San Bernardino 92404   714-883-8701
406
California Motorcycle Dealers Association
2210 K St., Suite D
Sacramento 95816   916-441-5296
407
California Moving and Storage Association
1206 Maple Ave.
Los Angeles 90015   213-746-1400
408
California Moving and Storage Association
2025 Gateway Pl., Suite 474
San Jose 95110   408-286-6553
409
California Music Merchants Association
128 E. 14th St.
Oakland 94606   415-893-3634
410
California Mutual Water Companies Associa-
    tion
101 E. Olive Ave.
Redlands 92373   714-793-4901

411
California - Nevada Hereford Association
P.O. Box 126
Clovis 93612　　　　　　　　209-299-6429

412
California Newspaper Publishers Association
1127 11th St., Suite 1040
Sacramento 95814　　　　　　916-443-5991

413
California Newspaper Publishers Association
707 S. Hill St.
Los Angeles 90014　　　　　　213-627-0160

414
California Newspaper Publishers Association
657 Mission St.
San Francisco 94105　　　　　415-392-0259

415
California Nurses Association
790 Market St.
San Francisco 94102　　　　　415-986-2220

416
California Nurses Association
1543 W. Olympic Blvd.
Los Angeles 90015　　　　　　213-385-6281

417
California Nurses Association
921 11th St., Suite 902
Sacramento 95814　　　　　　916-446-5019

418
California Off Track Betting Committee
2422 E St.
Sacramento 95816　　　　　　916-442-0600

419
California Olive Association
c/o Canners League of California
1007 L St.
Sacramento 95814　　　　　　916-444-9260

420
California Optometric Association
921 11th St.
P.O. Box 2591
Sacramento 95814　　　　　　916-441-3990

421
California Optometric Association
3459 Cahuenga Blvd. W.
Los Angeles 90068　　　　　　213-874-0600

422
California Orthotics and Prosthetics
  Association
1117 Market St.
San Francisco 94103　　　　　415-621-4244
　　(Artificial limbs and corrective devices.)

423
California Park and Recreation Society
1400 K St., Suite 302
Sacramento 95814　　　　　　916-441-0254

424
California Peace Officers Association
1107 9th St., Suite 800
Sacramento 95814　　　　　　916-446-7847

425
California Personnel and Guidance Association
654 E. Commonwealth
Fullerton 92631　　　　　　　714-871-6460

426
California Pharmaceutical Academy of Community Practice
1030 N. Maclay Ave.
San Fernando 91340　　　　　213-365-9173

427
California Pharmacists - Political Action
  Committee
555 Capitol Mall
Sacramento 95814　　　　　　916-444-7811

428
California Podiatry Association
26 O'Farrell St.
San Francisco 94108　　　　　415-781-2387

429
California Police Chiefs Association
Forum Building
1107 9th St.
Sacramento 95814　　　　　　916-442-6503

430
California Polled Hereford Association
12385 Jahant Rd.
Acampo 95220　　　　　　　　209-369-3477

431
California Pork Producers Association
2855 Telegraph Ave.
Berkeley 94705　　　　　　　415-644-7151

432
California Potato Growers
P.O. Box 1328
Shafter 93263　　　　　　　　805-746-4951

433
California Potato Research Advisory Board
200 New Stine Rd., Suite 131
Bakersfield 93303　　　　　　805-834-6685

434
California Practical Nurses Association
535 E. Vine
West Covina 91790　　　　　　213-338-4416

435
California Press Photographers Association
P.O. Box 191
San Diego 92112
436
California Probation, Parole and Correction-
al Association
1722 J St., Suite 18
Sacramento 95814   916-442-4721
437
California Professional Horseman's
Association
P.O. Box L
Elk Grove 95624   916-682-2101
438
California Prune Advisory Board
103 World Trade Center
San Francisco 94111   415-986-1452
439
California Psychiatric Association
2232 Carleton St.
Berkeley 94704   415-848-5330
440
California Psychiatric Association
1107 9th St.
Sacramento 95814   916-443-1596
441
California Public Defenders Association
850 Bryant St., Room 205
San Francisco 94103
442
California Public Defenders Association
717 K St., Suite 500
Sacramento 95814   916-448-1383
443
California Public Health Association
693 Sutter St.
San Francisco 94102   415-673-7266
444
California Purebread Dairy Cattle Association
Merced College
Merced 95340   209-723-4321
445
California Radiological Society
1225 8th St., Suite 590
Sacramento 95814   916-446-2028
446
California Railroad Association
1127 11th St., Suite 242
Sacramento 95814   916-448-3381
447
California Raisin Advisory Board
3636 N. First, Suite 148
Fresno 93755   209-224-7010

448
California Rare Fruit Growers
Star Route P.O. Box P
Bonsall 92003   714-758-0054
449
California Redwood Association
617 Montgomery St.
San Francisco 94111   415-392-7880
450
California Refuse Removal Council
3972 N. Waterman, Suite 106
San Bernardino 92404   714-883-8701
451
California Refuse Removal Council
Forum Building
1107 9th St., Suite 700
Sacramento 95814   916-446-4025
452
California Retail Hardware Association
122 9th St.
San Francisco 94103   415-552-0536
453
California Retail Liquor Dealers Association
1713 J St., Suite 2
Sacramento 95814   916-444-9800
454
California Retailers Association
1127 11th St., Suite 1030
Sacramento 95814   916-443-1975
455
California Retired Teachers Association
268 E. 12th
Oakland 94606   415-763-4021
456
California Rice Growers Association
901 South River Rd.
West Sacramento 95691   916-371-6941
457
California Savings and Loan League
9800 S. Sepulveda Blvd., Suite 500
Los Angeles 90045   213-670-6300
458
California Savings and Loan League
925 L St., Suite 780
Sacramento 95814   916-443-5955
459
California School Bus Contractors Association
2271 Tulip Way
Sacramento 95821   916-922-2788
460
California School Employees Association
1543 W. Olympic Blvd.
Los Angeles 90015   213-381-5672

461
California Seafood Institute
11th and L Building, Suite 1003
Sacramento 95814 916-447-4068

462
California Seed Association
510 Bercut Dr., Suite H
Sacramento 95814 916-441-2251

463
California Seed Council
c/o California Department of Food and
 Agriculture
1220 N St.
Sacramento 95814 916-445-2388

464
California Self Insurers Association
1107 9th St., Suite 519
Sacramento 95814 916-442-4576

465
California Service Station Association
1224 Contra Costa Blvd.
Pleasant Hill 94523 415-825-0514

466
California Sheep Dog Society
P.O. Box 251
Dixon 95620 916-678-2556

467
California Society of Anesthesiologists
100 S. Ellsworth Ave., Suite 806
San Mateo 94401 415-348-1407

468
California Society of Certified Public
 Accountants
100 Welch Rd.
Palo Alto 94304 415-321-9545

469
California Society of Certified Public
 Accountants
2600 Wilshire
Los Angeles 90057 213-385-1744

470
California Society of Farm Managers and
 Rural Appraisers
c/o Department of Agricultural Economics
University of California
Davis 95616 916-752-1531

471
California Society of Internal Medicine
703 Market St.
San Francisco 94103 415-362-1548

472
California Society of Pathologists
1225 8th St., Suite 590
Sacramento 95814 916-446-6001

473
California Society of Professional Engineers
160 Sansome St.
San Francisco 94104 415-421-3184

474
California Society of Professional Engineers
1107 9th St.
Sacramento 95814 916-442-1041

475
California Speech and Hearing Association
1801 Vicente
P.O. Box 16205
San Francisco 94116 415-665-7881

476
California State Association of Barbers and
 Beauticians
650 S. Spring St.
Los Angeles 90014 213-622-6233

477
California State Beekeepers Association
24634 W. Manning
San Joaquin 93660

478
California State Bowling Association
1146 S. Inglewood Ave.
Inglewood 90301 213-678-7739

479
California State Builders Exchange
1111 Howe Ave., Suite 225
Sacramento 95825 916-929-4382

480
California State Club Association
1000 California St.
San Francisco 94108 415-775-1234
  (League of private clubs.)

481
California State Dairy Goat Council
4450 Wise Rd.
Lincoln 95648

482
California State Electronics Association
13666 S. Hawthorne Blvd.
Hawthorne 90250 213-679-9186

483
California State Employees Association
4949 Wilshire Blvd.
Los Angeles 90010 213-938-9121

484
California State Employees Association
1108 O St.
Sacramento 95814 916-444-8134

485
California State Firemen's Association, Inc.
926 J St., Suite 616
Sacramento 95814　　　　　916-441-4153
486
California State Florists Association
651 Brannan St.
San Francisco 94107　　　　415-495-6780
487
California State Grange
2101 Stockton Blvd.
Sacramento 95817　　　　　916-455-2656
488
California State Horsemen's Association
P.O. Box 1179
Santa Rosa 95402　　　　　707-544-2252
489
California State Hypnosis Association
7060 Hollywood Blvd.
Los Angeles 90046　　　　　213-461-1133
490
California State Park Rangers Association
1275 Sunnycrest Ave.
Ventura 93003　　　　　　　805-642-6352
491
California State Sheriffs Association
1107 9th St., Suite 800
Sacramento 95814　　　　　916-446-0667
492
California State Spiritualist Association
7066 Hawthorn Ave.
Los Angeles 90028　　　　　213-469-1336
493
California State Tire Dealers Association
303 Hegenberger Rd.
Oakland 94621　　　　　　　415-562-0594
494
California Strawberry Advisory Board
P.O. Box 269
Watsonville 95076　　　　　408-724-1301
495
California Stripper Well Association
2975 Wilshire Blvd.
Los Angeles 90010　　　　　213-383-0763
　　(Wells that produce relatively small
　　quantities of oil)
496
California Swap Meet Owners Association
120 N. Robertson Blvd.
Los Angeles 90048　　　　　213-657-8420
497
California Sweet Potato Growers Association
5475 N. Arena Way
Livingston 95334　　　　　　290-394-7935

498
California Swimming Pool Industry Energy,
　Codes and Legislative Council
220 Montgomery St., Suite 1405
San Francisco 94104　　　　415-391-8080
499
California Taxicab Owners Association
1107 9th St., Suite 819
Sacramento 95814　　　　　916-441-0393
500
California Taxpayers Association
921 11th, Suite 800
Sacramento 95814　　　　　916-441-0490
　　(Business - supported political action
　　group that works to control state gover-
　　ment expenditures.)
501
California Taxpayers Association
612 S. Flower, Suite 309
Los Angeles 90017　　　　　213-627-9001
502
California Teachers Association
State Headquarters
1705 Murchison Dr.
Burlingame 94010　　　　　415-697-1400
503
California Teachers Association
1125 W. 6th St.
Los Angeles 90017　　　　　213-482-5660
504
California Teachers Association
Governmental Relations Office
1127 11th St.
Sacramento 95814　　　　　916-442-5895
505
California Thoroughbred Breeders Association
201 Colorado Pl.
Arcadia 91006　　　　　　　213-445-7800
506
California Thoroughbred Farm Managers
　Association
13171 6th St.
Chino 91710
507
California Tomato Growers
9036 Thornton Rd.
Stockton 95207　　　　　　　209-478-1761
508
California Tomato Research Institute
9036 Thornton Rd.
Stockton 95207　　　　　　　209-478-1761

509
California Trial Lawyers Association
1020 12th St.
Sacramento 95814   916-442-6902
510
California Trucking Association
1240 Bayshore Highway
Burlingame 94010   415-347-3651
511
California Trucking Association
6055 E. Washington Blvd.
Los Angeles 90040   213-685-6868
512
California Trucking Association
1127 11th St.
Sacramento 95814   916-442-1017
513
California Turkey Industry Board
814 14th St., Room 3
P.O. Box 3329
Modesto 95353   209-529-6055
514
California Valley Exports
17 Drumm St.
San Francisco 94111   415-362-6649
515
California Veterinary Medical Association
1024 Country Club Dr.
Moraga 94556   415-376-2020
516
California Warehousemen's Association
220 Montgomery St., Suite 1405
San Francisco 94104   415-391-8080
517
California Water Resources Association
245 E. Olive
Burbank 91502   213-849-3129
518
California Westside Farmers
Security Bank Building
1060 Fulton Mall, Suite 1115
Fresno 93721   209-485-9180
519
California Women for Agriculture
P.O. Box 88
Santa Paula 93060   805-525-1907
520
California Wool Growers Association
3382 El Camino Ave., Suite 6
Sacramento 95821   916-482-9680
521
Cal/Nev Electrical Contractors
1110 2nd St.
Sacramento 95814   916-444-3770

522
Cal - Western Appaloosa Racings, Inc.
P.O. Box 185
Clovis 93612   209-299-1444
523
Cal - Wool Marketing Association
P.O. Box 1108
Stockton 95201   209-466-6866
524
Canners League of California
1007 L St.
Sacramento 95814   916-444-9260
525
Cash and Carry Dairy Association of Southern
   California
19922 Pioneer Blvd.
Cerritos 90701   213-865-4406
526
Cast Iron Soil Pipe Foundation
P.O. Box 452
Los Angeles 90028   213-464-7341
527
Ceramic Tile Institute
700 N. Virgil Ave.
Los Angeles 90029   213-660-1911
528
Certified Contractors Association
   (Out of business.)
529
Chamber of Commerce of the United States
100 Park Center Plaza
San Jose 95113   408-275-8110
530
Chefs' Association of the Pacific Coast, Inc.
995 Market St.
San Francisco 94103   415-495-7080
531
Chefs de Cuisine Association of California
607 S. Park View Ave.
Los Angeles 90057   213-385-2941
532
Chinese Bay Area Apparel Contractors
   Association
1235 Stockton
San Francisco 94133   415-989-1907
533
Chinese Chamber of Commerce
425 Gin Ling Way
Los Angeles 90012   213-628-1828
534
Chinese Laundry Association
33 Spofford
San Francisco 94108   415-982-3409

535
Chinese Librarians Association
P.O. Box 2688
Stanford 94305

536
Chinese Produce Merchants Association
943 1/2 S. San Pedro St.
Los Angeles 90015   213-622-9916

537
Chrysler Plymouth Dealers Association, Los
  Angeles Region
1601 Gower Ave.
Los Angeles 90028   213-467-7139

538
Citrus Men's Clubs
26715 Avenue 140
Porterville 93257   209-784-5852

539
Citrus Research Board
117 W. 9th St., Room 913
Los Angeles 90015   213-627-3041

540
City Hostess International
2523 J St., Suite 6
Sacramento 95816   916-444-5896

541
City Service Truck Owners Association of
  Los Angeles
766 N. Virgil Ave.
Los Angeles 90029   213-660-2707

542
Classroom Teachers Association of Los
  Angeles
1125 W. 6th St.
Los Angeles 90017   213-481-0420

543
Cling Peach Advisory Board
1 California St., 11th Floor
San Francisco 94111   415-982-0970

544
Coalition of Apparel Industries in California
110 E. 9th St., Suite A-361
Los Angeles 90015   213-627-1034

545
Code Authority of the National Association of
  Broadcasters
7060 Hollywood Blvd., Suite 511
Los Angeles 90028   213-462-6909

546
College Band Directors National Association
59 Student Center
University of California
Berkeley 94720   415-642-3436

547
Commercial Fishermen of California
233 A St.
San Diego 92101   714-234-1961

548
Committee of Small Magazine Editors and
  Publishers
P.O. Box 703
San Francisco 94101   415-776-1943

549
Composers and Lyricists Guild of America
10999 Riverside
North Hollywood 91602   213-985-4102

550
Concrete Masonry Association of California
  and Nevada
1824 Tribute Road, Suite J
Sacramento 95815   916-920-4414

551
Concrete Pumpers Association
606 N. Larchmont Blvd.
Los Angeles 90004   213-467-1158

552
Concrete Sawing and Drilling Association
606 N. Larchmont Blvd., Suite 4-A
Los Angeles 90004   213-467-1158

553
Condominium Development Association
1134 Ballena Blvd.
Alameda 94501   415-521-1221

554
Congress of California Dermatological
  Societies
4955 Van Nuys Blvd.
Sherman Oaks 91403   213-981-8510

555
Congress of County Medical Societies
1233 Hermosa Ave.
Hermosa Beach 90254   213-372-6565

556
Conservation Committee of California Oil
  Producers
417 S. Hill St.
Los Angeles 90013   213-625-7731

557
Construction Industry Council of California
8301 Edgewater Dr.
Oakland 94621   415-638-2505

558
Construction Industry Legislative Council
926 J St.
Sacramento 95814   916-444-8240

559
Construction Industry Research Board
1625 W. Olympic Blvd.
Los Angeles 90015   213-381-6544
560
Construction Specifications Institute
6163 St. Albans St.
Los Angeles 90042   213-257-6564
561
Consumer Retail Services Trade Association
12345 Ventura Blvd.
Studio City 91604   213-877-5608
562
Consulting Engineers Association of California
433 Airport Blvd., Suite 303
Burlingame 94010   415-344-5782
563
Consulting Engineers Association of California
3467 Kurtz
San Diego 92110   714-224-2911
564
Contracting Plasterers Association of Southern California
5301 Laurel Canyon Rd.
North Hollywood 91607   213-877-2191
565
Contractors Bonding Association, Inc.
2216 Gladwick
Compton 90220   213-774-2276
566
Costume Designers Guild
11286 Westminster
Los Angeles 90066   213-397-3162
567
Council of Better Business Bureaus
1826 N. Sierra Bonita Ave.
Los Angeles 90046   213-876-4911
568
Council of Black Nurses
2431 W. 116th
Inglewood 90303   213-757-0828
569
Council of California Growers
520 S. El Camino Real
San Mateo 94402   415-347-6688
570
Council of Housing Producers
9255 Sunset Blvd.
Los Angeles 90069   213-550-8211

571
Coyote
P. O. Box 26354
San Francisco 94126   415-957-1610
     (Organization of prostitutes.)
572
Crab Boat Owners Association
2907 Jones St.
San Francisco 94133   415-885-1180
573
Credit Managers Association of Southern California
2300 W. Olympic Blvd.
Los Angeles 90006   213-381-2661
574
Credit Officers Group
932 W. Kenneth Rd.
Glendale 91202   213-245-3475
575
Cremation Association of North America
15300 Ventura Blvd., Suite 305
Sherman Oaks 91403   213-990-5966
576
Criminal Trial Lawyers Association
1255 Post St.
San Francisco 94109   415-673-3850
577
Cryogenic Society of America
1637 Chelsea Rd.
Palos Verdes Estates 90274   213-378-0528
578
Cuban National Bar Association
3806 Beverly Blvd.
Los Angeles 90004   213-385-4726
579
Dairy Council of California
2775 Cottage Way, Suite 19
Sacramento 95825   916-445-8790
580
Dairy Employer's Association of California
1225 8th St., Suite 385
Sacramento 95814   916-444-5674
581
Dairy Institute of California
11th and L Building, Suite 718
Sacramento 95814   916-441-6921
582
Dairymen's Service Association
P. O. Box 53
Riverside 92502   714-783-0111
583
Data Processing Management Association
P. O. Box 625
San Francisco 94104   415-397-4644

584
Date Administrative Committee
81 - 855 Highway 111, Room 2-G
Indio 92201   714-347-4510

585
Date Growers' Institute
81-855 Highway111, Room 2-G
Indio 92201   714-347-4510

586
Dehydrated and Convenience Foods Council
P.O. Box 801
Healdsburg 95448   707-433-1864

587
Dental Foundation of California
1856 Pandora Ave.
Los Angeles 90025   213-933-6887

588
Desert Grape Advisory Board
1677 Sixth St.
Coachella 92236   714-398-5622
    (Office open May - August)

589
DFA of California
303 Brokaw Rd.
P.O. Box 270 A
Santa Clara 95052   408-241-9302
    (Dried fruit and tree nut industry.)

590
Diamond - Sunsweet, Inc.
P.O. Box 1727
Stockton 95201   209-466-4851
    (Consolidation of marketing operations of
    Diamond Walnut Growers, Inc., and
    Sunsweet Growers, Inc.)

591
Diamond Walnut Growers
1050 S. Diamond St.
P.O. Box 1727
Stockton 95201   209-466-4851
    (Marketing cooperative with some 3,000
    California members.)

592
Dichondra Council
P.O. Box 1428
Woodland 95695   916-662-1763

593
Direct Marketing Club of Southern California
1801 S. Hill
Los Angeles 90015   213-747-3735

594
Directors Guild of America
7950 Sunset Blvd.
Hollywood 90046   213-656-1220

595
Dried Fig Advisory Board
1000 Topeka Ave.
Fresno 93712   209-264-5011

596
Dry Bean Advisory Board
P.O. Box 943
Dinuba 93618   209-591-4866

597
Drywall Industry Trust Fund
520 S. Virgil Ave.
Los Angeles 90020   213-380-9132

598
Egg Advisory Board
600 N. Mountain Ave., Suite A-104
Upland 91786   714-981-4923

599
Electric Club of Los Angeles
1052 W. 6th St.
Los Angeles 90011   213-481-0898

600
Electric and Gas Industries Association
1355 Market St.
San Francisco 94102   415-431-6030

601
Electrical Contractors of California/Nevada
1110 2nd St.
Sacramento 95814   916-444-3770

602
Electrical Industries Association of Southern
    California
9911 W. Pico
Los Angeles 90035   213-556-0513

603
Electrical Industry Depository of California
1355 Market St.
San Francisco 94103   415-621-4312

604
Electrical Maintenance Engineers Association
    of California
3500 Pertita Ave.
Los Angeles 90039   213-663-2800

605
Electrical Training Trust
1313 W 8th, Suite 208
Los Angeles 90017   213-483-0104
    (Selection and training of workers in the
    Los Angeles County electrical construc-
    tion industry.)

606
Electronic Representative Association of
    Southern California
23999 Ventura Blvd.
Calabsas 91302   213-888-9908

607
Electronic Representative Association of
  Southern California
23999 Ventura Blvd.
Calabasas 91302   213-888-9908
608
Employee Benefit Planning Association of
  Southern California
417 S. Hill St., Suite 1101
Los Angeles 90013   213-627-4691
609
Energy Products and Services Association
861 6th Ave.
San Diego 94122   714-233-3171
610
Engineering Contractors Association
8310 Florence Ave.
Downey 90240   213-861-0929
611
Engineering Contractors Association
1517 L St.
Sacramento 95814   916-443-8144
612
Engineering and General Contractors Associ-
  ation
6150 Mission Gorge Rd., Suite 215
San Diego 92120   714-280-7174
613
Engineering and Grading Contractors Associ-
  ation
1152 Red Pine Ct.
San Jose 95152   408-287-3422
614
Engineers and Architects Association
727 W. 7th
Los Angeles 90017   213-624-9317
615
Environmental Exporters Institute
691 Newdock St.
Terminal Island 90731   213-937-3500
616
Evangelical Press Association
P.O. Box 707
La Canada Flintridge 91011
617
Executives Association
Leamington Hotel
19th and Franklin
Oakland 94607   415-451-7670
618
Executives Association
770 B St.
San Diego 92101   714-233-8195

619
Executive Association of San Francisco
637 Market St.
San Francisco 94105   415-781-6461
620
Exposition Management Association
c/o William S. Orkin
2220 Avenue of the Stars
Los Angeles 90067   213-277-0800
621
Faculty Association of the California
  Community Colleges
926 J St.
Sacramento 95814   916-447-3865
622
Far East Merchants Association
1597 Curtis St.
Berkeley 94702   415-527-3455
623
Far West Ski Association
3325 Wilshire Blvd., Suite 1340
Los Angeles 90010   213-387-2145
624
Fashion Group, Inc.
117 W. 9th St., Suite 826
Los Angeles 90015   213-489-2920
625
Federated Dairymen
660 W. 17th St.
Merced 95340   209-722-7583
626
Federated Employers of the Bay Area
582 Market St.
San Francisco 94105   415-982-2018
627
Federation of California Racing Associations,
  Inc.
P.O. Box 369
Inglewood 90306   213-678-1181
628
Film Advisory Board
1727 N. Sycamore
Hollywood 90028   213-874-3644
629
Film and Television Coordinating Committee
c/o Mac St. Johns
Publicists Guild
1427 N. La Brea Ave.
Los Angeles 90028   213-851-1600
630
Flying Dentists Association
5820 Wilshire Blvd., Suite 500
Los Angeles 90036   213-937-5514

631
Flying Psychologists
190 N. Oakland Ave.
Pasadena 91101   213-795-5144
632
Food Employers Council
2599 S. Flower St.
Los Angeles 90007   213-749-9301
633
Food Processors Institute
1950 Sixth St.
Berkeley 94710   415-548-6670
634
Foreign Trade Association of Southern California
350 S. Figueroa St.
Los Angeles 90071   213-627-0634
635
Forest Landowners of California
1851 Heritage Ln., Suite 181
Sacramento 95815   916-929-5451
    (Non - industrial timberland owners.)
636
F. P. Association
8732 Sunset Blvd., Suite 206
Los Angeles 90069   213-657-1731
    (Foreign correspondents covering the
     movie industry.)
637
Fresh Market Tomato Advisory Board
200 New Stine Rd.
Bakersfield 93303   805-834-6544
638
Fresh Produce Council of Southern California
746 S. Central Ave.
Los Angeles 90021   213-623-3345
639
Friends of Books and Comics
330 Ellis St.
San Francisco 94102   415-775-0918
    (Publishers and others interested.)
640
Garment Contractors Association of Southern
  California
9171 Wilshire Blvd.
Beverly Hills 90210   213-273-8599
641
Gemological Institute of America
1660 Stewart St.
Santa Monica 90404   213-829-2991

642
German American Chamber of Commerce of
  Los Angeles
3250 Wilshire Blvd., Suite 2212
Los Angeles 90010   213-381-2236
643
German American Chamber of Commerce of
  the Pacific Coast
465 California St.
San Francisco 94104   415-392-2262
644
Golden State Walnut Growers Association
1405 8th St.
Modesto 95352   209-521-1194
645
Governmental Refuse Collection and Disposal
  Association
4001 Westerly Place
P.O. Box W
Newport Beach 92663   714-833-0512
646
Grapefruit Administrative Committee
3033 N. Central Ave., Room 509-A
Phoenix, Arizona 85012   602-265-2618
647
Grapefruit Advisory Board
3033 N. Central Ave.
Phoenix, Arizona 85012   602-265-2618
648
Greater Los Angeles Press Club
600 N. Vermont Ave.
Los Angeles 90004   213-665-1141
649
Gypsum Association
1800 N. Highland Blvd.
Los Angeles 90028   213-465-0663
650
Hearing Aid Association of California
1107 9th St., Room 220
Sacramento 95814   916-441-0108
651
Hebrew Master Bakers Association
12444 Victory Blvd., Suite 315
North Hollywood 91606   213-877-0545
652
Highway Carriers Association
1107 9th St., Suite 700
Sacramento 95814   916-446-4024
653
Highway Carriers Association
5110 District Blvd.
Maywood 90270   213-771-7711

HIGHWAY USERS FEDERATION   INSTITUTE OF REAL ESTATE MANAGEMENT

654
Highway Users Federation for Safety and
  Mobility
926 J St.
Sacramento 95814   916-443-5314
655
Hollywood Radio and Television Society
171 N. Highland Ave., Suite 618
Hollywood 90028   213-465-1183
656
Honey Advisory Board
13601 E. Whittier Blvd., Suite 511
Whittier 90608   213-698-5210
657
Horsemen's Benevolent Protective Associa-
  tion
Hollywood Park Office
P.O. Box 369
Inglewood 90306   213-677-7151
658
Hospital Council of Southern California
6255 W. Sunset Blvd.
Los Angeles 90028   213-469-7311
659
Hotel Employers' Council of Los Angeles
608 S. Hill St.
Los Angeles 90014   213-634-7761
660
Human Factors Society
P.O. Box 1369
Santa Monica 90406   213-394-1811
    (Concerned with the role of humans in
    complex systems.)
661
Iceberg Lettuce Research Program
2110 K St.
P.O. Box 160366
Sacramento 95816   916-441-7184
662
Imported Hardware Products Association, Inc.
50 California St.
San Francisco 94111   415-433-4878
663
Independent Automotive Dealers Association
  of California
1107 J St.
Sacramento 95814   916-441-6663
664
Independent Insurance Agents Association of
  California
465 California St.
San Francisco 94104   415-981-2714

665
Independent Insurance Agents and Brokers
Association of Los Angeles
1541 Wilshire Blvd.
Los Angeles 90017   213-483-3981
666
Independent Motion Picture Producers Associ-
  ation
6110 Santa Monica Blvd.
Hollywood 90038
667
Independent Refiners Association of California
900 Wilshire Blvd.
Los Angeles 90017   213-489-5555
668
Independent Truckers Association
No address available   213-466-6415
669
Industrial Caterers Association
4676 Admiralty Way
Marina Del Rey 90291   213-870-1391
670
Industrial Employers and Distributors
  Association
5801 Chrisitie Ave.
Emeryville 94608   415-653-6765
671
Industry Education Council of California
650 S. Spring St.
Los Angeles 90014   213-628-1014
672
Information Film Producers of America, Inc.
P.O. Box 1470
Hollywood 90028   213-465-4898
673
Institute of Electrical and Electronic
  Engineers
999 N. Sepulveda Blvd.
El Segundo 90049   213-772-0126
674
Institute of Food Technologists
2140 Shattuck Ave.
Berkeley 94707   415-848-0582
675
Institute of Heating and Air Conditioning
  Industries, Inc.
606 N. Larchmont Blvd.
Los Angeles 90004   213-467-1158
676
Institute of Real Estate Management
505 Shatto Pl.
Los Angeles 90020   213-380-7190

32

677
Insulation Contractors of California
1900 Point West Way, Suite 120
Sacramento 95815　　　　916-929-2275

678
Insurance Agents and Brokers Legislative
　Council
1127 11th St., Suite 518
Sacramento 95814　　　　916-446-1428

679
Insurance Brokers Association
5225 Wilshire Blvd.
Los Angeles 90036　　　　213-936-5229

680
Interment Association of California
925 L St., Room 315
Sacramento 95814　　　　916-441-4533

681
International Academy of Metabology
1000 E. Walnut St.
Pasadena 91106　　　　213-795-7772

682
International Academy of Trial Lawyers
Paseo Building, Suite 206
S. First St. at the Paseo de San Antonio
San Jose 95113　　　　408-275-6767

683
International Air Transport Association
530 W. 6th St.
Los Angeles 90014　　　　213-623-2004

684
International Association of Business Com-
　municators
878 Market St., Suite 928
San Francisco 94102　　　　415-433-3400

685
International Association of Credit Card
　Investigators
1620 Grant Ave.
Novato 94947　　　　415-897-8800

686
International Association of LV/LP Nurses,
　Inc.
1900 Avenue of the Stars, Room 2340
Los Angeles 90067　　　　213-552-1501
　　(Licensed vocational and practical
　　nurses.)

687
International Association of Plumbing and
　Mechanical Officials
5032 Alhambra Ave.
Los Angeles 90032　　　　213-223-1471

688
International Association of Trichologists
18645 Sherman Way, Room 208
Reseda 91335　　　　213-705-1808
　　(Concerned with hair and its diseases.)

689
International College of Applied Nutrition
P. O. Box 386
La Habra 90631　　　　213-697-4576

690
International Conference of Building Officials
5360 S. Workman Mill Rd.
Whittier 90601　　　　213-699-0541

691
International Doll Makers Association
3364 Pine Creek Dr.
San Jose 95132　　　　408-926-3077

692
International Drapery Association
1116 E. 12th St.
Los Angeles 90021　　　　213-625-8301

693
International Farmers Aid Assocation
1521 Larkin St.
San Francisco 94109　　　　415-775-8200

694
International Farmers Assocation for
　Education
2855 Telegraph Ave.
Berkeley 94705　　　　415-644-7099

695
International Fence Industry Association, Inc.
P. O. Box 9677
Sacramento 95823　　　　916-428-6472

696
International Institute for Lath and Plaster
9911 Inglewood Ave., Suite 205
Inglewood 90301　　　　213-671-7767

697
International Institute of Municipal Clerks
160 N. Altadena Dr.
Pasadena 91107　　　　213-795-6153

698
International Kart Federation, Inc.
416 S. Grand Ave.
Covina 91724　　　　213-967-4197

699
International Micrographic Congress
P. O. Box 22440
San Diego 92122　　　　714-278-4562

700
International Ministerial Federation
5290 N. Sherman Ave.
Fresno 93710　　　　209-222-9338

701
International Society for Labor Law and
  Social Security
U.S. National Branch
UCLA School of Law
Los Angeles 90024   213-825-1296
702
International Society of Mutual Benefits
506 15th St.
Oakland 94612   415-451-2737
703
International Transactional Analysis
  Association
1772 Vallejo St.
San Francisco 94123   415-885-5992
704
Interracial Council for Business Opportunity
2651 S. Western Ave., Suite 300
Los Angeles 90017
705
Inventors Assistance League
1815 W. 6th St.
Los Angeles 90057   213-483-4850
706
Inventors' Workshop International
16218 Ventura Blvd., Suite 4
Encino 91436   213-990-4140
707
Investigators and Process Servers Joint Leg-
  islative Committee
305 W 41st Ave.
San Mateo 94402   415-341-0060
708
Invest - in - America
Northern California Council
235 Montgomery St., Suite 1023
San Francisco 94104   415-781-3282
  (Public relations program to encourage
  voluntary savings by individuals.)
709
Invest - in - America
Southern California Council
800 Wilshire Blvd., Suite 777
Los Angeles 90017   213-623-4772
710
Japan Business Association of Southern
  California
350 S. Figueroa St.
Los Angeles 90071   213-628-1263
711
Japanese Chamber of Commerce
355 E. First St.
Los Angeles 90012   213-626-5116

712
Japanese Chamber of Commerce of Northern
  California
312 Sutter St.
San Francisco 94108   415-986-6140
713
Junior World Trade Association
465 California St.
San Francisco 94104   415-392-4511
714
Kiwi Growers of California
Route 1, Box 445
Chico 95926   916-345-9529
  (Commercial growers of kiwifruit, also
  known as Chinese gooseberries.)
715
Korean Traders Association of America
981 S. Western Ave.
Los Angeles 90006   213-735-5873
716
Lathing Contractors Association of Southern
  California
14039 Sherman Way
Van Nuys 91405   213-782-2012
717
Lathing Institute of Southern California
2801 West Temple St.
Los Angeles 90026   213-387-5161
718
Latin American Chamber of Commerce of
  Northern California
3000 Folsom St.
San Francisco 94110   415-826-0505
719
Latin American Teachers' Association
3800 Folsom St.
San Francisco 94110   415-824-2352
720
Lawyers Club of Los Angeles County
412 W. Sixth St.
Los Angeles 90014   213-622-8682
721
League of California Milk Producers
1225 8th St., Room 385
Sacramento 95814   916-444-5674
722
Lemon Administrative Committee
117 W. 9th St., Room 905
Los Angeles 90015   213-624-3403

723
Lepidopterists' Society
c/o Julian P. Donahue
Los Angeles County Museum of Natural
  History
900 Exposition Blvd.
Los Angeles 90007   213-744-3364
724
Life Underwriters Association of Los Angeles
417 S. Hill St.
Los Angeles 90013   213-627-4691
725
Los Angeles Bowling Association
4250 Melrose Ave.
Los Angeles 90029   213-663-8109
726
Los Angeles Coat and Suit Contractors Association
117 W. 9th St.
Los Angeles 90015   213-489-1015
727
Los Angeles Copyright Society
c/o Ziffren and Ziffren
10889 Wilshire Blvd., Suite 1260
Los Angeles 90024   213-272-6557
728
Los Angeles General Agents and Managers
  Association
417 S. Hill St.
Los Angeles 90013   213-627-4691
729
Los Angeles Grain Exchange
3415 N. Fletcher Ave., Suite 5
El Monte 91731   213-443-8937
730
Los Angeles Machinery Distributors Association
4430 Sheila
Los Angeles 90023   213-263-9887
731
Los Angeles Steamship Association
350 S. Figueroa St., Suite 226
Los Angeles 90071   213-627-0634
732
Los Angeles Trial Lawyers Association
1730 W. Olympic Blvd.
Los Angeles 90015   213-487-1212
733
Lumber Association of Southern California
1915 Beverly Blvd.
Los Angeles 90057   213-483-6450

734
Lumber Merchants Association of Northern
  California
1055 Lincoln Ave.
San Jose 95125   408-295-4103
735
Manufactured Housing Institute
3855 E. La Palma Ave.
Anaheim 92807   714-630-1440
736
Manufacturers' Agents National Association
P.O. Box 16878
Irvine 92713   714-752-5231
737
Manufacturers Shipping Association
4430 Sheila
Los Angeles 90023   213-263-9881
738
Manufacturing Milk Producers Advisory Board
1213 13th St.
Modesto 95352   209-521-1060
739
Marina and Recreation Association
P.O. Box 156
Antioch 94509   415-757-9449
740
Marine Exchange of Los Angeles - Long Beach
  Harbor, Inc.
P.O. Box 2524
Long Beach 90801   213-432-0813
  (Records and disseminates information
  on arrivals and departures of commercial
  vessels.)
741
Marine Technology Society
615 S. Flower St.
Los Angeles 90017   213-620-1703
742
Marshals Association of California
P.O. Box 2921
San Diego 92112   714-236-3424
743
Masonry Advisory and Technical Institute
22300 Foothill Blvd.
Hayward 94541   415-538-7307
744
Masonry Industry Advancement Committee
2550 Beverly Blvd.
Los Angeles 90057   213-382-1347
745
Masonry Institute
55 New Montgomery St.
San Francisco 94105   415-781-7642

746
Masonry Institute of America
2550 Beverly Blvd.
Los Angeles 90057   213-388-0472
747
Masters, Mates and Pilots Offshore - Pacific
1025 Howard St.
San Francisco 94103   415-861-3600
748
Meat Dealers Association of Southern
  California
403 W. 8th St.
Los Angeles 90014   213-622-1632
749
Meat Distributors, Inc.
4330 Alcoa Ave.
Los Angeles 90058   213-583-4205
750
Meat Packers, Inc.
2930 E. 44th St.
Los Angeles 90058   213-588-7195
751
Meat Purveyors Service
2833 Leonis Blvd.
Los Angeles 90058   213-581-8133
752
Mechanical Contractors Association of
  Northern California, Inc.
1410 Irving
San Francisco 94122   415-661-4994
753
Medical Correctional Association
339 N. Oakhurst Dr.
Beverly Hills 90210   213-274-2141
754
Melon Research Board
200 New Stine Rd., Suite 131
Bakersfield 93303   805-834-5896
755
Mens Apparel Guild in California
124 E. Olympic Blvd.
Los Angeles 90015   213-746-0623
756
Merchants and Manufacturers Association
1150 S. Olive St.
Los Angeles 90015   213-748-0421
    (Also known as M & M Association.)
757
Metal Finishing Association of Southern
  California, Inc.
5820 Wilshire Blvd., Suite 500
Los Angeles 90036   213-245-1510

758
Milk Producers Council
13545 Euclid Ave.
Ontairo 91761   714-628-6018
759
Minority Contractors Association of Los
  Angeles
945 S. Western Ave.
Los Angeles 90006   213-737-7952
760
Minority Contractors Association of Northern
  California
303 Hegenberger Rd., Room 408-A
Oakland 94621   415-632-4138
761
Motion Picture and Television Credit
  Association
1725 Beverly Blvd.
Los Angeles 90026   213-483-4694
762
Motion Picture and Television Fund
335 N. La Brea Ave.
Los Angeles 90036   213-937-7250
763
Motion Picture Association of America
8480 Beverly Blvd.
Los Angeles 90048   213-653-2200
764
Motor Car Dealers Association of Southern
  California
1801 Avenue of the Stars, Suite 650
Los Angeles 90067   213-277-0091
765
Motorcycle Industry Council
4100 Birch St., Suite 101
Newport Beach 92660   714-752-7833
766
Motor Vehicle Manufactures Association
1225 8th St., Suite 300
Sacramento 95814   916-444-3767
767
Multi/National Business Association
1441 S. Beverly Glen Blvd.
Los Angeles 90024   213-474-2538
768
Music Teachers Association of California
12 Geary St.
San Francisco 94108   415-392-3340
769
National Academy of Recording Arts and
  Sciences
4444 Riverside Dr.
Burbank 91505   213-843-8233

770
National Alliance of Black School Educators
P.O. Box 22613
Sacramento 95831   916-927-3614
771
National Alliance of Business
450 Grand Ave., Room G 106
Los Angeles 90012   213-626-5121
   (Formerly: National Alliance of Business-
   men. Major organization working to help
   the economically disadvantaged through
   jobs, training, and other services.)
772
National Alliance of Business
433 California St.
San Francisco 94104   415-421-9660
773
National Association of Accountants
530 W. 6th St.
Los Angeles 90014   213-624-6400
774
National Association of Bank Women
333 S. Hope St.
Los Angeles 90012   213-620-0132
775
National Association of Broadcasters
606 N. Larchmont Blvd.
Los Angeles 90004   213-462-6909
776
National Association of Business Economists,
   Los Angeles Chapter
c/o T.A. Gibson, President
Rockwell International Corporation - AB 90
12214 Lakewood Blvd.
Downey 90241   213-687-6425
777
National Association of Civil Service Employ-
ees
P.O. Box 19463
San Diego 92119   714-464-1191
778
National Association of Computerized Tax
   Processors
c/o Itel - Tacs
7330 N. Figueroa St.
Los Angeles 90041   213-772-2502
779
National Association of Credit Management
4215 Freeport Blvd.
Sacramento 95822   916-451-8416
780
National Association of Electrical Distributors
315 W. 9th St.
Los Angeles 90015   213-622-0056

781
National Association of Enrolled Agents
16100 Ventura Blvd., Room 8
Encino 91436   213-784-0561
   (Persons enrolled to practice before the
   Internal Revenue Service.)
782
National Association of Human Services
   Technologies
1127 11th St., Main Floor
Sacramento 95814   916-444-3772
783
National Association of Language Laboratory
   Directors
University of California
Irvine 92664   714-833-5011
784
National Association of Manufacturers
601 N. Vermont
Los Angeles 90005   213-665-5971
785
National Association of Negro Business and
   Professional Women's Clubs
760 Market St.
San Francisco 94102   415-397-6240
786
National Association of Physical Therapists
P.O. Box 367
West Covina 91793   213-331-4066
787
National Association of Principals of Schools
   for Girls
910 Lathrop Dr.
Stanford 94305   415-326-2672
788
National Association of Progressive Radio
   Announcers, Inc.
2020 N. Las Palmas Ave.
Los Angeles 90068   213-464-1419
789
National Association of Reporter Training
   Schools
3580 Aero Ct.
San Diego 92123   714-560-0222
790
National Association of Securities Dealers
425 California St.
San Francisco 94104   415-781-3434
791
National Association of Seventh-Day Adventist
   Dentists
c/o Dr. Don L. Beglau
P.O. Box 101
Loma Linda 95423   714-797-5660

792
National Association of Social Workers
California Chapter
11th and L Building, Suite 431
Sacramento 95814   916-442-0485
793
National Association of Social Workers
6223 Selma Ave.
Los Angeles 90028   213-461-8206
794
National Associational of Spanish Speaking
  Librarians
c/o Chicano Research Library
405 Hilgard Ave.
Los Angeles 90024   213-825-2105
795
National Association of Underwater Instruc-
  tors
P.O. Box 630
Colton 92324   714-824-5440
796
National Association of Women in Construc-
  tion
No address available   916-487-1897
797
National Automatic Merchandising Association
10889 Wilshire Blvd.
Los Angeles 90024   213-477-5547
798
National Automotive Muffler Association
P.O. Box 1857
West Covina 91793   213-338-2417
799
National Bicycle Association
1107 9th St., Suite 700
Sacramento 95814
800
National Canners Association
1950 6th St.
Berkeley 94710   415-843-9762
801
National Clay Pipe Institute
Western Regional Office
14700 E. Firestone, Suite 111
La Mirada 90638   213-387-5171
802
National College of Foot Surgeons
c/o Dr. A. Apkarian
22030 Sherman Way
Canoga Park 91303   213-340-1713
803
National Concrete Masonry Association
55 New Montgomery St.
San Francisco 94105   415-781-7642

804
National Conference of Bankruptcy Judges
P.O. Box 2070
Oakland 94604   415-451-7687
805
National Conference of Personal Managers
c/o Conference of Personal Managers, West
9220 W. Sunset Blvd.
Los Angeles 90069   213-273-3060
806
National Educators Fellowship
1410 W. Colorado Blvd.
Pasadena 91105   213-684-1881
807
National Electrical Contractors Association,
  Los Angeles County
2408 S. Broadway
Los Angeles 90007   213-748-5587
808
National Electronic Distributors Association
9363 Wilshire Blvd., Suite 211
Beverly Hills 90210   213-278-0543
809
National Federation of Independent Business
National Office
150 W. 20th Ave.
San Mateo 94403   415-341-7441
    (Major group that lobbies at state and
    federal levels for the interests of
    independent business.)
810
National Federation of Independent Business
3205 Valencia Hill
Riverside 92507   714-781-6673
811
National Fire Protection Association
10050 N. Wolfe Rd.
Cupertino 95014   408-446-9889
812
National Garden Bureau
4546 El Camino Real, Suite A
Los Altos 94022   415-941-2030
    (Industry - funded program to help
    professional writers on gardening.)
813
National Guard Association of California
1013 58th St.
Sacramento 95819   916-457-0176
814
National Lawyers Guild
712 S. Grandview Ave.
Los Angeles 90057   213-380-3180
    (Political - legal organization.)

815
National Motel Brokers
P.O. Box 5446
San Mateo 94402   415-349-1234

816
National Notary Association
23012 Ventura Blvd.
Woodland Hills 91364   213-347-2035

817
National Nutritional Foods Association
7727 S. Painter Ave.
Whittier 90602   213-945-2669

818
National Order of Women Legislators
810 San Vicente Blvd.
Santa Monica 90402   213-394-2270

819
National Public Parks Tennis Association
155 W. Washington Blvd.
Los Angeles 90015   213-749-6941

820
National Recreation and Park Association
1400 K St., Suite 302
Sacramento 95814   916-441-0445

821
National Safflower Council
111 Sutter St., Suite 1333
San Francisco 94104   415-392-5718

822
National Secretaries Association
3600 Wilshire Blvd.
Los Angeles 90010   213-389-1312

823
National Secretaries Association
1021 McKinley Ave.
Oakland 94610   415-832-0276

824
National Sporting Goods Association
8060 E. Florence
Downey 90240   213-861-9794

825
National Surf Life Saving Association of
   America
P.O. Box 366
Huntington Beach 92648   714-536-2581

826
National Swimming Pool Institute
220 Montgomery St.
San Francisco 94104   415-391-8080

827
National Water Supply Improvement Associ-
   ation
P.O. Box 8300
Fountain Valley 92708   714-556-8260

828
National Worm Growers Association
8889 Carlisle Ave.
Sacramento 95828   916-682-7862

829
Newspaper Advertising Sales Association
3660 Wilshire Blvd.
Los Angeles 90010   213-483-6595

830
Non - Commissioned Officers Association
2475 Cordova Lane
Rancho Cordova 95670   916-635-4805

831
Northern California Carnation Growers
   Association
10 Adrian Ct.
Burlingame 94010   415-692-5008

832
Northern California Concrete Masonry
   Association
55 New Montgomery St.
San Francisco 94105   415-781-7642

833
Northern California Dental Laboratory
   Association
5801 Christie Ave.
Emeryville 94608   415-655-9579

834
Northern California Grocers Association
4163 Piedmont Ave.
Oakland 94611   415-655-3854

835
Northern California Grocers Association
1807 Tribute Rd.
Sacramento 95815   916-929-9741

836
Northern California Hotel and Motel Association
1826 Noriega
San Francisco 94122   415-564-3781

837
Northern California Marine Association
380 Embarcadero, West
Oakland 94607   415-834-1215

838
Northern California Milk Container Exchange
855 29th St.
Oakland 94608   415-444-8922

839
Northern California Motor Car Dealers
1244 Larkin St.
San Francisco 94109   415-673-5346

840
Northern California Professional Horsemen's
  Association
720 Northgate Rd.
Walnut Creek 94598
841
Northern California Psychiatric Society
No address available   415-334-0133
842
Northern California Restaurant Association
No longer in operation
843
Northern California Route Operators
  Association
1846 Rollins Rd.
Burlingame 94010
844
Northern California State Dental Hygienists'
  Association
220 Montgomery St., Suite 1405
San Francisco 94104   415-391-8080
845
Northern California Suppliers Association
369 Pine
San Francisco 94104   415-781-8604
846
Northern California Thoroughbred Association
P.O. Box 3008
Santa Rosa 95403   707-539-1655
847
Northern California Worm Growers Associa-
  tion
970 Piner Rd.
P.O. Box 6043
Santa Rosa 95406   707-544-5575
848
Occupational Therapy Association of Califor-
  nia
c/o Esther D. Wayne, Executive Director
P.O. Box 17792
Irvine 92713   714-559-0947
849
Officers for Justice - Peace Officers Assoc-
  iation
5126 3rd St.
San Francisco 94122   415-822-2225
850
Olive Administrative Committee
516 N. Fulton St.
Fresno 93728   209-486-1383
851
Orange Administrative Committees
117 W. 9th St.,Room 913
Los Angeles 90015   213-627-3041

852
Oregon - California Potato Marketing Comm-
  ittee
Equitable Building, Suite 214
530 Center St., N.E.
Salem, Oregon 97301   503-378-5423
853
Organization of Women Executives
5900 Wilshire Blvd.
Los Angeles 90036   213-933-7337
854
Osteopathic Physicians and Suregons of
  California
No address available   213-389-6574
855
Overseas Craftsmen's Association
2061 Business Center Dr.
Irvine 92664   714-833-9477
856
Pacific Area Travel Association
228 Grant Ave.
San Francisco 94108   415-986-4646
    (Major international organization of
    governments and businesses.)
857
Pacific Coast Coffee Association
465 California St., Suite 722
San Francisco 94104   415-986-0267
858
Pacific Coast Electrical Association
1545 Wilshire Blvd.
Los Angeles 90017   213-483-3891
859
Pacific Coast Federation of Fishermen's
  Associations, Inc.
P.O. Box 1626
Sausalito 94965   415-332-5080
860
Pacific Coast Gas Association
1650 S. Amphiett Blvd.
San Mateo 94401   415-573-1893
861
Pacific Coast Meat Jobbers Association
995 Market St.
San Francisco 94103   415-986-4547
862
Pacific Coast Showman's Association
1235 S. Hope St.
Los Angeles 90015   213-747-2002
863
Pacific Coast Quarter Horse Racing Associ-
  ation
3662 Katella Ave., Suite 102
Los Alamitos 90720   213-598-8718

864
Pacific Coast Tire Dealers Association
905 N. Euclid., Suite H
Anaheim 92803   714-774-0187
865
Pacific Contractors Association
3550 Wilshire Blvd., Suite 20000
Los Angeles 90010   213-385-5211
866
Pacific Cruise Conference
311 California St.
San Francisco 94104   415-981-5370
867
Pacific Egg and Poultry Association
5420 W. Jefferson Blvd.
Los Angeles 90016   213-938-2675
868
Pacific International Worm Growers Coop.
16450 Washington
Riverside 92504   714-780-2888
869
Pacific Maritime Association
635 Sacramento
San Francisco 94111   415-362-7973
    (Shipping industry labor relations
    organization.)
870
Pacific Merchant Shipping Association
P.O. Box 7861
San Francisco 94120   415-986-7900
871
Pacific Southwest Distributors Association
1800 N. Argyle Ave., Suite 510
Los Angeles 90028   213-469-2229
    (Plumbing and heating.)
872
Pacific Southwest Hardware Association
117 S. Clementine St.
Anaheim 92805   714-778-2050
873
Pacific Stock Exchange
618 S. Spring St.
Los Angeles 90014   213-627-8741
874
Pacific Water Conditioning Association
2041 Business Center Dr., Suite 214
Irvine 92664   714-833-3131
875
Pacific Water Conditioning Contractors of
    California
1900 Point West Way, Room 198
Sacramento 95815   916-929-5207

876
Paint and Wallpaper Association of Southern
    California
2352 W. 3rd St.
Los Angeles 90057   213-383-1228
877
Painting and Decorating Contractors Associ-
    ation
1777 Vine
Los Angeles 90028   213-461-3548
878
Parking and Highway Improvement Contrac-
    tors Association
606 N. Larchmont Blvd.
Los Angeles 90004   213-467-1158
879
Peace Officers Research Association of
    California
Senator Hotel
Sacramento 95814   916-442-5081
880
Pear Growers League
2292 Elkhorn Ct.
P.O. Box 458
San Jose 95125   408-248-8200
881
Pear Program Committee
P.O. Box 255383
Sacramento 95825   916-483-9261
882
Peninsula Manufacturers Association
3921 E. Bayshore Rd.
Palo Alto 94303   408-965-2436
883
Permanent Charities Committee of the
    Entertainment Industries
463 N. La Cienega Blvd.
Los Angeles 90048   213-652-4680
884
Personnel and Industrial Relations Associ-
    ation, Inc.
1730 W. Olympic Blvd.
Los Angeles 90015   213-384-1221
885
Pest Control Operators of California, Inc.
3444 W. First St.
Los Angeles 90004   213-386-1034
886
Pharmaceutical Manufacturers Association
No longer maintains an office in California

887
Photo Engravers Association of Southern
California
1434 W. 12th St.
Los Angeles 90015   213-747-5521

888
Planning Executives Institute
Los Angeles Chapter
1010 Wilshire Blvd.
Los Angeles 90017   213-621-7708

889
Plastic Pipe Institute
611 S. Catalina Ave.
Los Angeles 90005   213-381-1630

890
Plumbing, Heating and Cooling Contractors
Association
1434 Howe Ave., Suite 92
Sacramento 95825   916-922-1006

891
Plumbing and Piping Industry Council
501 Shatto Place
Los Angeles 90020   213-487-3790

892
Portland Cement, Inc.
P.O. Box 60513 TA
Los Angeles 90060   213-386-8450

893
Press Club of San Francisco
555 Post St.
San Francisco 94102   415-775-7800

894
Printing Industries Association
1434 W. 12th St.
Los Angeles 90019   213-747-5521

895
Printing Industries of Northern California
168 2nd St.
San Francisco 94105   415-781-8242

896
Private Truck Owners Bureau of California
947 Markham Ct.
Eldorado Hills 95630   916-446-7889

897
Processing Strawberry Advisory Board of
California
251 E. Lake Ave., Suite 8
Watsonville 95076   408-724-5454

898
Processing Tomato Advisory Board
1757 Barcelona St.
Livermore 94550   415-447-1738

899
Processors Clingstone Peach Advisory
Board
1 California St.
San Francisco 94111   415-982-0970

900
Producers Canning Cling Advisory Board
1 California St.
San Francisco 94111   415-982-0970

901
Producers' Council, Inc.
1052 W. 6th St.
Los Angeles 90017   213-481-0060

902
Producers Guild of America
8201 Beverly Blvd.
Los Angeles 90048   213-651-0084

903
Producers Livestock Marketing Association
c/o Los Angeles Producers Stockyard
10750 Riverside Dr.
Ontario 91761   714-983-5891

904
Production Engine Remanufacturers Association
1800 N. Argyle Ave., Suite 510
Hollywood 90028   213-469-8966

905
Professional Air Traffic Controllers Organization
333 Hegenberger Rd.
Oakland 94621   415-562-8450

906
Professional Association of Diving Instructors
2064 N. Bush St.
Santa Ana 92706   714-547-6996

907
Professional Educators Group of California
555 Capitol Mall, Suite 440
Sacramento 95814   916-446-6561

908
Professional Educators of Los Angeles
4525 Sherman Oaks Ave.
Sherman Oaks 91403   213-872-1350

909
Professional Engineers in California Govern-
ment
2717 Cottage Way, Suite 14
Sacramento 95825   916-488-0461

910
Professional Horsemen's Association of
America
P.O. Box 1047
Rancho Santa Fe 92067   714-756-2749

911
Professional Painting Contractors Association
P.O. Box 5515
San Jose 95150   408-265-7870
912
Professional Photographers of California
319 Pacific Ave.
San Francisco 94111   415-391-2895
913
Professional Woman's Center
P.O. Box 17828
San Diego 92117   714-292-5842
914
Professional Women's Alliance
1125 Taylor St.
San Francisco 94108   415-775-3137
915
Propeller Club of the United States -
   Port of Los Angeles-Long Beach
350 S. Figueroa St., Suite 226
Los Angeles 90071   213-620-3300
      (Maritime civic organization that works to
      support the U.S. Merchant Marine.)
916
Prune Administrative Committee
World Trade Center, Room 103
San Francisco 94111   415-986-5190
917
Public Agency Risk Managers Association
5750 Almaden Expressway
San Jose 95118   408-265-2600
918
Public Relations Society of America
Southern California Chapter
1533 Wilshire Blvd.
Los Angeles 90017   213-483-8375
919
Pulp and Paper Traffic League
c/o Crown Zellerbach Corporation
1 Bush St.
San Francisco 94119   415-823-5000
920
Purchasing Management Association of
   Northern California, Inc.
870 Market St.
San Francisco 94102   415-392-1600
921
Purebread Sheep Breeders Society
3585 S. West Ave.
Fresno 93706
922
Radio Advertising Bureau, Inc.
1900 Avenue of the Stars
Los Angeles 90067   213-553-9479

923
Radio and Television News Association of
   Southern California
1741 N. Ivar St., Suite 204
Los Angeles 90028   213-462-6371
924
Raisin Administrative Committee
P.O. Box 231
Fresno 93708   209-225-0520
925
Recording Industry Association of America
9200 Sunset Blvd.
Los Angeles 90069   213-278-5500
926
Recreation Vehicle Dealers Association
1107 9th St., Suite 700
Sacramento 95814   916-446-4024
927
Recreation Vehicle Industry Association
Western Region Office
1748 W. Katella Ave., Suite 206
Orange 92667   714-532-1688
928
Restaurant Association of Southern California
448 S. Hill St.
Los Angeles 90071   213-628-3371
929
Restaurant Hotel Employers Council of
   Southern California
608 S. Hill St.
Los Angeles 90014   213-624-7761
930
Restaurant Safety Association
c/o Pacific States Financial Corporation
2691 W. 9th St.
Los Angeles 90006   213-387-3278
931
Retail Furniture Association of California
1355 Market St.
San Francisco 94102   415-861-5021
932
Rice Growers Association of California
P.O. Box 958
Sacramento 95804   916-371-6941
933
Rice Research Board
335 Teegarden St.
Yuba City 95991   916-673-6247
934
Roof Contractors Association of Southern
   California
11401 Valley Blvd.
El Monte 91731   213-579-1276

935
Roofing Contractors Industry Fund
11401 Valley Blvd.
El Monte 91731   213-444-7318
936
Safe Association
7252 Remmet Ave., Suite 203
Canoga Park 91303   213-340-3961
937
Safety Helmet Council of America
9841 Airport Blvd., Suite 1208
Los Angeles 90045   213-670-5811
938
Sales and Marketing Executives Association of
  Los Angeles
515 S. Olive St., Room 1-206
Los Angeles 90013   213-626-9465
939
Scaffold Industry Association
14309 Sherman Way
Van Nuys 91405   213-782-2012
940
Screen Actors Guild
7750 Sunset Blvd.
Hollywood 90046   213-876-3030
941
Screen Cartoonists Guild
1616 W. 9th St., Room 222
Los Angeles 90015   213-380-9860
942
Screen Composers of America
16255 Ventura Blvd., Suite 411
Encino 91436   213-986-9476
943
Screen Extras Guild
3629 Cahuenga Blvd., W.
Hollywood 90068   213-851-4301
944
Securities Industry Association
California District
160 Sansome St., 6th Floor
San Francisco 94104   415-392-7700
945
Security Equipment Industry Association
3310 Airport Ave.
Santa Monica 90405   213-390-8756
946
Seismological Society of America
2620 Telegraph Ave.
Berkeley 94704   415-848-0954
947
Semiconductor Industry Association
20380 Town Center Lane
Cupertino 95014   408-255-3522

948
Serve Yourself and Multiple Pump Association
3959 W. 6th St.
Los Angeles 90020   213-387-3114
949
Sheet Metal and Air Conditioning Contractors
  Association of Southern California
3130 Wilshire Blvd.
Los Angeles 90010   213-385-2297
950
Sign Users Council of California
100 S. Ellsworth
San Mateo 94401   415-343-9652
951
Society for Adolescent Medicine
P.O. Box 3462
Granda Hills 91344   213-368-5996
952
Society for Clinical Social Work
1107 9th St.
Sacramento 95814   916-441-1155
953
Society for History Education
California State University, Long Beach
Long Beach 90840   213-498-4431
954
Society for Information Display
654 N. Sepulveda Blvd.
Los Angeles 90049   213-472-3550
955
Society for Nutrition Education
2140 Shattuck Ave., Suite 1110
Berkeley 94704   415-548-1363
956
Society for Personality Assessment
1070 E. Angeleno Ave.
Burbank 91501
957
Society for Public Health Education
693 Sutter St., 4th Floor
San Francisco 94102   415-673-7266
958
Society for the Advancement of Material and
  Process Engineering
P.O. Box 613
Azusa 91702   213-334-1810
959
Society of Allied Weight Engineers
P.O. Box 60024, Terminal Annex
Los Angeles 90060   213-427-8262
960
Society of American Military Engineers
P.O. Box 174
Los Angeles 90053   213-688-5334

961
Society of American Value Engineers
1052 W. 6th St.
Los Angeles 90017   213-481-0880
962
Society of Biological Psychiatry
2010 Wilshire Blvd.
Los Angeles 90057   213-483-7863
963
Society of California Accountants
2131 Capitol Ave.
Sacramento 95816   916-443-2057
964
Society of California Non - Fiction Writers
118 Marywood Ave.
Claremont 91711   714-624-0362
965
Society of Certified Data Processors
4410 Glacier
San Diego 92120   714-280-3550
966
Society of Children's Book Writers
P.O. Box 296
Los Angeles 90066
967
Society of Exchange Counselors
P.O. Box 812
Glendora 91740   213-963-5959
    (Realtors who specialize in trading
    properties.)
968
Society of Experimental Test Pilots
P.O. Box 986
Lancaster 93534   805-942-9574
969
Society of Governmental Appraisers
536 Cedarberry Lane
San Rafael 94903   415-479-8978
970
Society of Insurance Brokers
22 Battery
San Francisco 94111   415-392-1625
971
Society of Motion Picture and Television Art
   Directors
7715 Sunset Blvd.
Hollywood 90046   213-876-4330
972
Society of Real Estate Appraisers
10850 Riverside Dr., Suite 400
Hollywood 91602   213-877-3809

973
Society of Research Administrators
c/o University of California
Los Angeles 90024   213-825-4243
974
Society of the Plastics Industry
611 S. Catalina St.
Los Angeles 90005   213-381-7787
975
Society of Vector Ecologists
3827 W. Chapman Ave.
Orange 92668   714-971-2421
976
Southern California Association of Cabinet
   Manufacturers
1933 S. Broadway
Los Angeles 90007   213-749-4355
977
Southern California Association of Civil
   Engineers and Land Surveyors
608 S. Hill St.
Los Angeles 90014   213-624-7761
978
Southern California Association of Industrial
   Nurses
No address available   213-484-1030
979
Southern California Broadcasters Association
1800 N. Highland Ave.
Los Angeles 90028   213-446-4481
980
Southern California Businessmen's Association
727 W. 7th St.
Los Angeles 90017   213-624-7739
981
Southern California Cattlemen's Association
8551 Hereford Dr.
Chino 91710   714-597-3737
982
Southern California Cleaners and Dyers
   Association
11401 Vanowen St.
North Hollywood 91605   213-766-3949
983
Southern California Contractors Association
4418 Beverly Blvd.
Los Angeles 90004   213-661-2141
984
Southern California Corporate Planners
   Association
c/o School of Business and Economics
California State University, Los Angeles
Los Angeles 90032   213-799-0881

985
Southern California Datsun Dealers
  Association, Inc.
6430 Sunset Blvd., Room 1117
Los Angeles 90028   213-464-7528
986
Southern California Dental Laboratory
  Association
3333 Glendale Blvd.
Los Angeles 90039   213-661-2188
987
Southern California Electric Sign Association
311 N. Normandie Ave.
Los Angeles 90004   213-666-5111
988
Southern California Floral Association
756 Wall St.
Los Angeles 90014   213-627-1201
989
Southern California Gardeners Federation
333 S. San Pedro St.
Los Angeles 90013   213-628-1595
990
Southern California Golf Association
3740 Cahuenga Blvd., W.
Studio City 91604   213-877-0901
991
Southern California Grocers Association
1636 W. 8th St.
Los Angeles 90017   213-381-5811
992
Southern California Industrial Editors
  Association
c/o Norris Industries
5215 S. Boyle Ave.
Los Angeles 90005   213-588-7111
993
Southern California Industrial Safety Society
3388 W. 8th St.
Los Angeles 90005   213-385-6461
994
Southern California Marine Association, Inc.
3711 Long Beach Blvd., Suite 405
Long Beach 90807   213-595-4364
995
Southern California Motion Picture Council
1727 N. Sycamore Ave.
Hollywood 90028   213-874-3644
996
Southern California Nisei Farmers League
P.O. Box 447
Encinitas 92027   714-436-3704

997
Southern California Office Machine Dealers
  Association
5300 Santa Monica Blvd.
Los Angeles 90029   213-467-9436
998
Southern California Paint and Coatings
  Association, Inc.
1021 1/2 S. Baldwin Ave.
Arcadia 91006   213-446-3240
999
Southern California Plastering Institute
1901 W. 8th St.
Los Angeles 90057   213-483-5932
1000
Southern California Professional Engineering
  Association
3711 Long Beach Blvd., Suite 903
Long Beach 90807   213-595-4548
1001
Southern California Plywood Association
2975 Wilshire Blvd.
Los Angeles 90010   213-387-1919
1002
Southern California Racing Association
4961 E. Katella Ave.
Los Alamitos 90720   213-431-1361
1003
Southern California Ready Mixed Concrete
  Association
P.O. Box 40
South Pasadena 91030   213-441-3107
1004
Southern California Restaurant Association
448 S. Hill St.
Los Angeles 90013   213-628-3371
1005
Southern California Retail Liquor Dealers
  Association
601 N. Vermont Ave.
Los Angeles 90005   213-666-7570
1006
Southern California Rock Products Association
P.O. Box 40
South Pasadena 91030   213-441-3106
1007
Southern California Society of Association
  Executives
14724 Ventura Blvd., Suite 604
Sherman Oaks 91403   213-986-8066
1008
Southern California Society of Oral Surgeons
P.O. Box 967
San Gabriel 91778   213-285-3733

1009
Southern California Tire Dealers and
  Retreaders Association
905 N. Euclid Ave., Suite H
Anaheim 92801   714-774-0117
1010
Specialty Advertising Association of
  California
5820 Wilshire Blvd.
Los Angeles   213-272-7623
1011
Specialty Equipment Manufacturers
  Association
11001 E. Valley Mall, Suite 200
El Monte 91731   213-579-1225
1012
Squab Producers of California
23682 Clawiter Rd.
Hayward 94545   415-785-0344
1013
State Bar of California
555 Franklin St.
San Francisco 94102   415-561-8200
1014
State Bar of California
1230 W. 3rd St.
Los Angeles 90033   213-482-4040
1015
State of California Auto Dismantlers
  Association
535 E. Vine St.
West Covina 91790   213-337-8215
1016
Stockbrokers Society
4311 Wilshire Blvd.
Los Angeles 90010   213-937-8300
1017
Stockbrokers Society
24 California St.
San Francisco 94111   415-421-7044
1018
Strawberry Advisory Board
255-A E. Lake
Watsonville 95076   408-724-1301
1019
Structural Engineers Association of
  California
171 Second St.
San Francisco 94105   415-362-1721
1020
Structural Engineers Association of Southern
  California
2208 Beverly Blvd.
Los Angeles 90057   213-385-4424

1021
Stucco Manifacturers Association
14006 Ventura Blvd.
Sherman Oaks 91423   213-789-8733
1022
Student Insurance Producers Association
P.O. Box 7372
Stockton 95207   209-951-2853
1023
Studio Publicity Directors' Committee
8480 Beverly Blvd.
Los Angeles 90048   213-653-2200
1024
Stuntmen's Association of Motion Pictures
4810 Whitsett Ave.
North Hollywood 91607   213-984-0806
1025
Sunkist Growers, Inc.
P.O. Box 7888
Van Nuys 91409   213-986-4800
  (Marketing cooperative of 7,300 citrus
  growers in California and Arizona.)
1026
Sun - Maid Raisin Growers of California
13525 S. Bethel Ave.
Kingsburg 93631   209-897-5861
1027
Sunsweet Growers
1050 S. Diamond St.
P.O. Box 1727
Stockton 95201   209-466-4851
  (Marketing cooperative of 900 California
  growers of dried prunes, apricots,
  peaches, pears and apples.)
1028
Sweet Potato Council of California
c/o Merced County Fram Bureau
646 S. Los Banos Highway
Merced 95340   209-723-3001
1029
System Safety Society
P.O. Box A
Newport Beach 92663   213-820-4441
  (Members are those who avoid design
  features and materials that provide
  hazards during use of systems.)
1030
Technical Marketing Society of America
P.O. Box 91113
Los Angeles 90009   213-649-2426
  (Professionals in the field of advanced
  programs and new business procurement
  in high technology industries.)

1031
Technology Transfer Society
11720 West Pico Blvd.
Los Angeles 90064   213-477-5081
1032
Tele-Communications Association
6311 Yucca St.
Los Angeles 90028
1033
Television Bureau of Advertising
3700 Wilshire Blvd.
Los Angeles 90010   213-380-8821
1034
Terrazzo Mosaic Association of Northern
  California
201 Golden Gate Ave.
San Francisco 94102   415-863-3071
1035
Textile Association of Los Angeles
819 Santee St.
Los Angeles 90014   213-627-6173
1036
Timber Operators Council
P.O. Box 41307
Sacramento 95814   916-966-8626
1037
Timber Operators Council
5330 Primrose Dr., Suite 138
Fair Oaks 95608
1038
Traffic Managers Conference of California
5455 Wilshire Blvd.
Los Angeles 90036   213-931-4073
1039
Trust for Automotive Political Education
2222 Sierra Blvd.
Sacramento 95825   916-929-9621
1040
Trust for Business Education
P.O. Box 30
Claremont 91711   714-624-0362
1041
Unemployment Insurance Association
P.O. Box 1138
Sacramento 95805   916-448-2003
1042
Union of American Physicians
World Trade Center, Suite 231 - 236
San Francisco 94111   415-391-9341
1043
United Business League
21250 California St., Suite 110
Woodland Hills 91367   213-999-3950

1044
United Dairymen's Association
14058 S. Euclid Ave.
Chino 91710   714-983-3692
1045
United Farmers and Ranchers of America
5110 E. Clinton Way, Suite 221
Fresno 93727   209-251-9837
1046
United Hospital Association
2049 Century Park, E., Suite 3201
Los Angeles 90067   213-277-7123
    (Spokesman for investor-owned taxpaying
    specialty and acute general hospitals in
    California.)
1047
United Inventors and Scientists of America
14431 Chase St.
Panorama City 91402   213-988-9320
1048
United Professors of California
901 F St., Suite 210
Sacramento 95814   916-442-1025
1049
United States Air Racing Association
16425 Hart St., Room 104
Van Nuys 91406   213-988-1751
1050
United States Brewers Association
235 Montgomery St.
San Francisco 94104   415-421-7747
1051
Universal Detective Association
P.O. Box 8180
Universal City 91608   213-848-5513
1052
Wallcovering Installers Association
14724 Ventura Blvd., Suite 604
Sherman Oaks 91403   213-986-8066
1053
Walnut Marketing Board
155 Bovet Rd.
San Mateo 94402   415-345-1631
1054
Waterbed Manufacturers Association
1411 W. Olympic Blvd.
Los Angeles 90015   213-384-3179
1055
Waterbed Retailers Association
14724 Ventura Blvd., Suite 604
Sherman Oaks 91403   213-986-8066

1056
Weather Modification Association
P. O. Box 490
Coronado 92118   714-435-5600
1057
West Coast Building Materials Dealers
 Association
950 Fulton Ave.
Sacramento 95825   916-483-9221
1058
West Coast Metal Importers Association, Inc.
350 S. Flower St., Room 226
Los Angeles 90071   213-627-0634
1059
West Coast Metal Importers Association, Inc.
303 World Trade Center
San Francisco 94111   415-986-5698
1060
Western Agricultural Chemicals Association
3120 0 St.
Sacramento 95816   916-455-9611
1061
Western America Convention and Travel
 Institute
Ceased operations 1978
1062
Western Association of Food Chains
640 Hilton Office Tower
Pasadena 91101   213-792-1143
1063
Western Association of Insurance Brokers
5225 Wilshire Blvd.
Los Angeles 90036   213-936-5229
1064
Western Association of Insurance Brokers
235 Montgomery St., Room 962
San Francisco 94104   415-392-5383
1065
Western Association of Schools and Colleges
1614 Rollins Rd.
Burlingame 94010   415-697-7711
1066
Western Association of Venture Capitalists
244 California St., Room 700
San Francisco 94111   415-781-6897
   (Formerly: Western Association of Small
   Business Investment Companies.)
1067
Western Association of Visual Merchandising
No address available   415-431-1234
1068
Western Awning Association
9911 Inglewood Ave., Suite 205
Inglewood 90301   213-671-7767

1069
Western Candy Conference
2086 Midwick Dr.
Altadena 91001   213-759-9165
1070
Western Coffee Association
1411 W. Olympic Blvd.
Los Angeles 90015   213-384-3179
1071
Western College Association
P. O. Box 9990
Mills College
Oakland 94613   415-632-5000
1072
Western Concrete Reinforcing Steel Institute
1499 Bayshore Hwy.
Burlingame 94010   415-697-1437
1073
Western Cotton Growers Association
c/o Kenneth E. Frick
Route 1 Box 318
Arvin 93203   805-854-2726
1074
Western Dairymen's Association
660 W. 17th St., Room 25
Merced 95340   209-722-7583
1075
Western Dental Society
8939 S. Sepulveda Blvd.
Los Angeles 90045   213-641-5561
1076
Western Electronics Manufacturers (WEMA)
2600 El Camino Real
Palo Alto 94306   415-327-9300
1077
Western Fairs Association
2500 Stockton Blvd.
P. O. Box 160448
Sacramento 95817   916-451-8478
1078
Western Fish Boat Owners Association
5055 N. Harbor Dr.
San Diego 92106   714-224-2475
1079
Western Floorcovering Association
333 N. Glenoaks Blvd., Suite 675
Burbank 91502   213-849-5019
1080
Western Forest Industries Association
1107 9th St.
Sacramento 95814   916-444-6395

1081
Western Growers Association
1811 Quail St.
Newport Beach 92663 714-833-8384
1082
Western Harness Racing, Inc.
P.O. Box 369
Inglewood 90306 213-678-1181
1083
Western Highway Institute
333 Pine St.
San Francisco 94104 415-986-4069
1084
Western Home Furnishings Association
1933 S. Broadway, Room 244
Los Angeles 90007 213-749-6197
1085
Western Hospital Association
830 Market St.
San Francisco 94102 415-421-8810
1086
Western Independent Bankers
1570 The Alameda, Suite 217
San Jose 95126 408-288-7650
1087
Western Liquid Gas Association
P.O. Box 356
Menlo Park 94025 415-325-1541
1088
Western Mobilehome Association
921 11th St., Room 1102
Sacramento 95814 916-444-8847
1089
Western Oil and Gas Association
727 W. 7th St., Suite 850
Los Angeles 90017 213-627-4866
1090
Western Office Machine Dealers Association
531 Mission St.
San Francisco 94105 415-495-3663
1091
Western Orothopedic Association
1970 Broadway
Oakland 94612 415-893-1257
1092
Western Paper Trade Association
14725 Ventura Blvd., Suite 604
Sherman Oaks 91403 213-986-8066
1093
Western Reprographics Association
1434 W. 12th St.
Los Angeles 90015 213-747-5521

1094
Western Roof Council
426 Pacific Ave.
San Francisco 94133 415-788-3431
1095
Western Society of Malacologists
15012 El Soneto Dr.
Whittier 90605 213-696-0687
1096
Western Society of Naturalists
c/o James M. Craig
Department of Biological Science
San Jose State University
San Jose 95192 408-277-3001
1097
Western Society of Periodontology
2626 Highland Ave.
Santa Monica 90405 213-399-1090
1098
Western Standardbred Association
1047 S. Prairie Ave., Room 5
Inglewood 90301 213-674-8246
1099
Western States Advertising Agencies
 Association
5900 Wilshire Blvd., Room 1402
Los Angeles 90036 213-933-7337
1100
Western States Ceramic Tile Contractors
 Association
5004 E. 59th Pl.
Maywood 90270 213-583-2421
1101
Western States Meat Packers Association
88 1st St.
San Francisco 94105 415-982-2466
1102
Western States Meat Packers Association
2930 E. 44th St.
Los Angeles 90058 213-588-7195
1103
Western Timber Association
211 Sutter St.
San Francisco 94108 415-956-0410
1104
Western Wholesale Pet Supply Association
4240 Gregory St.
Oakland 94619 415-530-2636
1105
Western Winter Sports Representatives'
 Association
685 Catamaran
Foster City 94404 415-349-5577

1106
Western Wood Products Association
6019 Blackbird Ct.
San Jose 95120   408-997-3615
    1107
Western Wooden Box Association
430 Sherman Ave., Suite 206
Palo Alto 94306   415-327-8200
    1108
Wine and Spirits Wholesalers of California
55 New Montgomery St.
San Francisco 94105   415-392-0125
    1109
Wine Institute
165 Post St.
San Francisco 94108   415-986-0878
    1110
Winter Pear Control Committee
601 Woodlark Building
Portland, Oregon 97205   503-223-8139
    1111
Women in Business
5900 Wilshire Blvd.
Los Angeles 90036   213-933-7300
    1112
Women in Communications, Inc.
1533 Wilshire Blvd., Suite 202
Los Angeles 90017   213-413-5014
    1113
Women in Timber
555 Capitol Mall, Suite 604
Sacramento 95814   916-443-9997
    1114
Women Library Workers
P.O. Box 9052
Berkeley 94709
    1115
Women's Veterinary Medical Association
c/o Dr. Donna Den Boer
29500 Heather Cliff Rd., Suite 38
Malibu 90265   213-347-0551
    1116
Woodwork Institute of California
1417 Georgia St.
Los Angeles 90015   213-749-8514
    1117
Woodwork Institute of California
850 S. Van Ness Ave.
San Francisco 94109   415-282-8220
    1118
Wool Bureau, Inc.
501 N. Sycamore Ave.
Los Angeles 90036   213-937-4843

1119
World Association of Detectives
P.O. Box 5068
San Mateo 94402   415-341-0060
    1120
World Dredging Association
P.O. Box 31
Long Beach 90801   213-432-6911
    1121
World Farm Foundation
2166 Garretson Ave.
Corona 91720   714-635-8333
    1122
Writers Guild of America, West
8955 Beverly Blvd.
Los Angeles 90048   213-550-1000

INDEX